MAXnotes®

William Shakespeare's

Henry V

Text by
Nick Pease
(Ph. D., SUNY Buffalo)
Department of Humanities
Polytechnic University
Hawthorne, New York

Illustrations by
Joseph Hornstein

Research & Education Association

MAXnotes® for
HENRY V

Printed in the United States of America

Library of Congress Catalog Card Number 96-67445

International Standard Book Number 0-87891-019-0

MAXnotes® is a registered trademark of
Research & Education Association, Piscataway, New Jersey 08854

What **MAXnotes**® *Will Do for You*

This book is intended to help you absorb the essential contents and features of William Shakespeare's *Henry V* and to help you gain a thorough understanding of the work. The book has been designed to do this more quickly and effectively than any other study guide.

For best results, this **MAXnotes** book should be used as a companion to the actual work, not instead of it. The interaction between the two will greatly benefit you.

To help you in your studies, this book presents the most up-to-date interpretations of every section of the actual work, followed by questions and fully explained answers that will enable you to analyze the material critically. The questions also will help you to test your understanding of the work and will prepare you for discussions and exams.

Meaningful illustrations are included to further enhance your understanding and enjoyment of the literary work. The illustrations are designed to place you into the mood and spirit of the work's settings.

The **MAXnotes** also include summaries, character lists, explanations of plot, and scene by scene analyses. A biography of the author and discussion of the work's historical context will help you put this literary piece into the proper perspective of what is taking place.

The use of this study guide will save you the hours of preparation time that would ordinarily be required to arrive at a complete grasp of this work of literature. You will be well prepared for classroom discussions, homework, and exams. The guidelines that are included for writing papers and reports on various topics will prepare you for any added work which may be assigned.

The **MAXnotes** will take your grades "to the max."

Dr. Max Fogiel
Program Director

Contents

> **Each Scene includes List of Characters,
> Summary, Analysis, Study Questions and
> Answers, and Suggested Essay Topics.**

SECTION ONE

Introduction

The Life and Work of William Shakespeare

The details of William Shakespeare's life are sketchy, mostly mere surmise based upon court or other clerical records. His parents, John and Mary (Arden), were married about 1557; she was of the landed gentry, and he was a yeoman—a glover and commodities merchant. By 1568, John had risen through the ranks of town government and held the position of high bailiff, which was a position similar to mayor. William, the eldest son and the third of eight children, was born in 1564, probably on April 23, several days before his baptism on April 26 in Stratford-upon-Avon. Shakespeare is also believed to have died on the same date—April 23—in 1616.

It is believed that William attended the local grammar school in Stratford where his parents lived, and that he studied primarily Latin, rhetoric, logic, and literature. Shakespeare probably left school at age 15, which was the norm, to take a job, especially since this was the period of his father's financial difficulty. At age 18 (1582), William married Anne Hathaway, a local farmer's daughter who was eight years his senior. Their first daughter (Susanna) was born six months later (1583), and twins Judith and Hamnet were born in 1585.

Shakespeare's life can be divided into three periods: the first 20 years in Stratford, which include his schooling, early marriage, and fatherhood; the next 25 years as an actor and playwright in London; and the last five in retirement in Stratford where he enjoyed moderate wealth gained from his theatrical successes. The years linking the first two periods are marked by a lack of information about Shakespeare, and are often referred to as the "dark years."

At some point during the "dark years," Shakespeare began his career with a London theatrical company, perhaps in 1589, for he was already an actor and playwright of some note by 1592. Shakespeare apparently wrote and acted for numerous theatrical companies, including Pembroke's Men, and Strange's Men, which later became the Chamberlain's Men, with whom he remained for the rest of his career.

In 1592, the Plague closed the theaters for about two years, and Shakespeare turned to writing book-length narrative poetry. Most notable were *Venus and Adonis* and *The Rape of Lucrece*, both of which were dedicated to the Earl of Southampton, whom scholars accept as Shakespeare's friend and benefactor despite a lack of documentation. During this same period, Shakespeare was writing his sonnets, which are more likely signs of the time's fashion rather than actual love poems detailing any particular relationship. He returned to playwriting when theaters reopened in 1594, and did not continue to write poetry. His sonnets were published without his consent in 1609, shortly before his retirement.

Amid all of his success, Shakespeare suffered the loss of his only son, Hamnet, who died in 1596 at the age of 11. But Shakespeare's career continued unabated, and in London in 1599, he became one of the partners in the new Globe Theater, which was built by the Chamberlain's Men.

Shakespeare wrote very little after 1612, which was the year he completed *Henry VIII*. It was during a performance of this play in 1613 that the Globe caught fire and burned to the ground. Sometime between 1610 and 1613, Shakespeare returned to Stratford, where he owned a large house and property, to spend his remaining years with his family.

William Shakespeare died on April 23, 1616, and was buried two days later in the chancel of Holy Trinity Church, where he had been baptized exactly 52 years earlier. His literary legacy included 37 plays, 154 sonnets, and five major poems.

Incredibly, most of Shakespeare's plays had never been published in anything except pamphlet form, and were simply extant as acting scripts stored at the Globe. Theater scripts were not regarded as literary works of art, but only the basis for the performance. Plays were simply a popular form of entertainment for all layers of society in Shakespeare's time. Only the efforts of two of Shakespeare's company, John Heminges and Henry Condell, preserved his 36 plays (minus *Pericles*, the thirty-seventh).

Shakespeare's Language

Shakespeare's language can create a strong pang of intimidation, even fear, in a large number of modern-day readers. Fortunately, however, this need not be the case. All that is needed to master the art of reading Shakespeare is to practice the techniques of unraveling uncommonly structured sentences and to become familiar with the poetic use of uncommon words. We must realize that during the 400-year span between Shakespeare's time and our own, both the way we live and speak has changed. Although most of his vocabulary is in use today, some of it is obsolete, and what may be most confusing is that some of his words are used today, but with slightly different or totally different meanings. On the stage, actors readily dissolve these language stumbling blocks. They study Shakespeare's dialogue and express it dramatically in word and in action so that its meaning is graphically enacted. If the reader studies Shakespeare's lines as an actor does, looking up and reflecting upon the meaning of unfamiliar words until real voice is discovered, he or she will suddenly experience the excitement, the depth, and the sheer poetry of what these characters say.

Shakespeare's Sentences

In English, or any other language, the meaning of a sentence greatly depends upon where each word is placed in that sentence. "The child hurt the mother" and "The mother hurt the child" have opposite meanings, even though the words are the same, simply because the words are arranged differently. Because word position is so integral to English, the reader will find unfamiliar word arrangements confusing, even difficult to understand. Since Shakespeare's plays are poetic dramas, he often shifts from average word arrangements to the strikingly unusual so that the line will conform to the desired poetic rhythm. Often, too, Shakespeare employs unusual word order to afford a character his own specific style of speaking.

Today, English sentence structure follows a sequence of subject first, verb second, and an optional object third. Shakespeare, however, often places the verb before the subject, which reads, "Speaks he" rather than "He speaks." Solanio speaks with this inverted structure in *The Merchant of Venice* stating, "I should be still/ Plucking the grass to know where sits the wind" (Bevington edition, I, i, ll.17-19), while today's standard English word order would have the clause at the end of this line read, "where the wind sits." "Wind" is the subject of this clause, and "sits" is the verb. Bassanio's words in Act Two also exemplify this inversion: "And in such eyes as ours appear not faults" (II, ii, l. 184). In our normal word order, we would say, "Faults do not appear in eyes such as ours," with "faults" as the subject in both Shakespeare's word order and ours.

Inversions like these are not troublesome, but when Shakespeare positions the predicate adjective or the object before the subject and verb, we are sometimes surprised. For example, rather than "I saw him," Shakespeare may use a structure such as "Him I saw." Similarly, "Cold the morning is" would be used for our "The morning is cold." Lady Macbeth demonstrates this inversion as she speaks of her husband: "Glamis thou art, and Cawdor, and shalt be/What thou art promised" (Macbeth, I, v, ll. 14-15). In current English word order, this quote would begin, "Thou art Glamis, and Cawdor."

In addition to inversions, Shakespeare purposefully keeps words apart that we generally keep together. To illustrate, consider Bassanio's humble admission in *The Merchant of Venice*: "I owe you much, and, like a wilful youth,/That which I owe is lost" (I, i, ll. 146-147). The phrase, "like a wilful youth," separates the regular sequence of "I owe you much" and "That which I owe is lost." To understand more clearly this type of passage, the reader could rearrange these word groups into our conventional order: I owe you much and I wasted what you gave me because I was young and impulsive. While these rearranged clauses will sound like normal English and will be simpler to understand, they will no longer have the desired poetic rhythm, and the emphasis will now be on the wrong words.

As we read Shakespeare, we will find words that are separated by long, interruptive statements. Often subjects are separated from verbs, and verbs are separated from objects. These long interruptions can be used to give a character dimension or to add an element of suspense. For example, in *Romeo and Juliet* Benvolio describes both Romeo's moodiness and his own sensitive and thoughtful nature:

> I, measuring his affections by my own,
> Which then most sought, where most might not be found,
> Being one too many by my weary self,
> Pursu'd my humour, not pursuing his,
> And gladly shunn'd who gladly fled from me.
> (I, i, ll. 126-130)

In this passage, the subject "I" is distanced from its verb "Pursu'd." The long interruption serves to provide information which is integral to the plot. Another example, taken from *Hamlet*, is the ghost, Hamlet's father, who describes Hamlet's uncle, Claudius, as

> . . . that incestuous, that adulterate beast,
> With witchcraft of his wit, with traitorous gifts—
> O wicked wit and gifts, that have the power
> So to seduce—won to his shameful lust
> The will of my most seeming virtuous queen.
> (I, v, ll. 43-47)

From this we learn that Prince Hamlet's mother is the victim of an evil seduction and deception. The delay between the subject, "beast," and the verb, "won," creates a moment of tension filled with the image of a cunning predator waiting for the right moment to spring into attack. This interruptive passage allows the play to unfold crucial information and thus to build the tension necessary to produce a riveting drama.

While at times these long delays are merely for decorative purposes, they are often used to narrate a particular situation or to enhance character development. As *Antony and Cleopatra* opens, an interruptive passage occurs in the first few lines. Although the delay is not lengthy, Philo's words vividly portray Antony's military prowess while they also reveal the immediate concern of the drama. Antony is distracted from his career and is now focused on Cleopatra:

>   . . . those goodly eyes,
> That o'er the files and musters of the war
> Have glow'd like plated Mars, now bend, now turn
> The office and devotion of their view
> Upon a tawny front. . . . (I, i, ll. 2-6)

Whereas Shakespeare sometimes heaps detail upon detail, his sentences are often elliptical, that is, they omit words we expect in written English sentences. In fact, we often do this in our spoken conversations. For instance, we say, "You see that?" when we really mean, "Did you see that?" Reading poetry or listening to lyrics in music conditions us to supply the omitted words and it makes us more comfortable reading this type of dialogue. Consider one passage in *The Merchant of Venice* where Antonio's friends ask him why he seems so sad and Solanio tells Antonio, "Why, then you are in love" (I, i, l. 46). When Antonio denies this, Solanio responds, "Not in love neither?" (I, i, l. 47). The word "you" is omitted but understood despite the confusing double negative.

In addition to leaving out words, Shakespeare often uses intentionally vague language, a strategy which taxes the reader's attentiveness. In *Antony and Cleopatra*, Cleopatra, upset that Antony is leaving for Rome after learning that his wife died in battle, convinces him to stay in Egypt:

> Sir, you and I must part, but that's not it:
> Sir you and I have lov'd, but there's not it;
> That you know well, something it is I would—
> O, my oblivion is a very Antony,
> And I am all forgotten.
> (I, iii, ll. 87-91, emphasis added)

In line 89, " . . . something it is I would" suggests that there is something that she would want to say, do, or have done. The intentional vagueness leaves us, and certainly Antony, to wonder. Though this sort of writing may appear lackadaisical for all that it leaves out, here the vagueness functions to portray Cleopatra as rhetorically sophisticated. Similarly, when asked what thing a crocodile is (meaning Antony himself who is being compared to a crocodile), Antony slyly evades the question by giving a vague reply:

> It is shap'd, sir, like itself, and it is as broad as it hath breadth. It is just so high as it is, and moves with it own organs. It lives by that which nourisheth it, and, the elements once out of it, it transmigrates.
> (II, vii, ll. 43-46)

This kind of evasiveness, or double-talk, occurs often in Shakespeare's writing and requires extra patience on the part of the reader.

Shakespeare's Words

As we read Shakespeare's plays, we will encounter uncommon words. Many of these words are not in use today. As *Romeo and Juliet* opens, we notice words like "shrift" (confession) and "holidame" (a holy relic). Words like these should be explained in notes to the text. Shakespeare also employs words which we still use, though with different meaning. For example, in *The Merchant of Venice* "caskets" refer to small, decorative chests for holding jewels. However, modern readers may think of a large cask instead of the smaller, diminutive casket.

Another trouble modern readers will have with Shakespeare's English is with words that are still in use today, but which mean something different in Elizabethan use. In *The Merchant of Venice*, Shakespeare uses the word "straight" (as in "straight away") where we would say "immediately." Here, the modern reader is unlikely to carry away the wrong message, however, since the modern meaning will simply make no sense. In this case, textual notes will clarify a phrase's meaning. To cite another example, in *Romeo and Juliet*, after Mercutio dies, Romeo states that the "black fate on moe days doth depend" (emphasis added). In this case, "depend" really means "impend."

Shakespeare's Wordplay

All of Shakespeare's works exhibit his mastery of playing with language and with such variety that many people have authored entire books on this subject alone. Shakespeare's most frequently

used types of wordplay are common: metaphors, similes, synecdoche and metonymy, personification, allusion, and puns. It is
when Shakespeare violates the normal use of these devices, or rhetorical figures, that the language becomes confusing.

A metaphor is a comparison in which an object or idea is re-
placed by another object or idea with common attributes. For example, in *Macbeth* a murderer tells Macbeth that Banquo has been
murdered, as directed, but that his son, Fleance, escaped, having
witnessed his father's murder. Fleance, now a threat to Macbeth,
is described as a serpent:

> There the grown serpent lies, the worm that's fled
> Hath nature that in time will venom breed,
> No teeth for the present. (III, iv, ll. 29-31, emphasis added)

Similes, on the other hand, compare objects or ideas while using
the words "like" or "as." In *Romeo and Juliet,* Romeo tells Juliet that
"Love goes toward love as schoolboys from their books" (II, ii, l.
156). Such similes often give way to more involved comparisons,
"extended similes." For example, Juliet tells Romeo:

> 'Tis almost morning, I would have thee gone,
> And yet no farther than a wonton's bird,
> That lets it hop a little from his hand
> Like a poor prisoner in his twisted gyves,
> And with silken thread plucks it back again,
> So loving-jealous of his liberty.
> (II, ii, ll. 176-181, emphasis added)

An epic simile, a device borrowed from heroic poetry, is an extended simile that builds into an even more elaborate comparison. In *Macbeth*, Macbeth describes King Duncan's virtues with an
angelic, celestial simile and then drives immediately into another
simile that redirects us into a vision of warfare and destruction:

> . . . Besides this Duncan
> Hath borne his faculties so meek, hath been
> So clear in his great office, that his virtues

> Will plead like angels, trumpet-tongued, against
> The deep damnation of his taking-off;
> And pity, like a naked new-born babe,
> Striding the blast, or heaven's cherubim, horsed
> Upon the sightless couriers of the air,
> Shall blow the horrid deed in every eye,
> That tears shall drown the wind. . . .
> (I, vii, ll. 16-25, emphasis added)

Shakespeare employs other devices, like synecdoche and metonymy, to achieve "verbal economy," or using one or two words to express more than one thought. Synecdoche is a figure of speech using a part for the whole. An example of synecdoche is using the word boards to imply a stage. Boards are only a small part of the materials that make up a stage, however, the term boards has become a colloquial synonym for stage. Metonymy is a figure of speech using the name of one thing for that of another which it is associated. An example of metonymy is using crown to mean the king (as used in the sentence "These lands belong to the crown"). Since a crown is associated with or an attribute of the king, the word crown has become a metonymy for the king. It is important to understand that every metonymy is a synecdoche, but not every synecdoche is a metonymy. This rule is true because a metonymy must not only be a part of the root word, making a synecdoche, but also be a unique attribute of or associated with the root word.

Synecdoche and metonymy in Shakespeare's works is often very confusing to a new student because he creates uses for words that they usually do not perform. This technique is often complicated and yet very subtle, which makes it difficult for a new student to dissect and understand. An example of these devices in one of Shakespeare's plays can be found in *The Merchant of Venice*. In warning his daughter, Jessica, to ignore the Christian revelries in the streets below, Shylock says:

> Lock up my doors; and when you hear the drum
> And the vile squealing of the wry-necked fife,
> Clamber not you up to the casements then . . .
> (I, v, ll. 30-32)

The phrase of importance in this quote is "the wry-necked fife." When a reader examines this phrase it does not seem to make sense; a fife is a cylinder-shaped instrument, there is no part of it that can be called a neck. The phrase then must be taken to refer to the fife-player, who has to twist his or her neck to play the fife. Fife, therefore, is a synecdoche for fife-player, much as boards is for stage. The trouble with understanding this phrase is that "vile squealing" logically refers to the sound of the fife, not the fife-player, and the reader might be led to take fife as the instrument because of the parallel reference to "drum" in the previous line. The best solution to this quandary is that Shakespeare uses the word fife to refer to both the instrument and the player. Both the player and the instrument are needed to complete the wordplay in this phrase, which, though difficult to understand to new readers, cannot be seen as a flaw since Shakespeare manages to convey two meanings with one word. This remarkable example of synecdoche illuminates Shakespeare's mastery of "verbal economy."

Shakespeare also uses vivid and imagistic wordplay through personification, in which human capacities and behaviors are attributed to inanimate objects. Bassanio, in *The Merchant of Venice*, almost speechless when Portia promises to marry him and share all her worldly wealth, states "my blood speaks to you in my veins . . . " (III, ii, l. 176). How deeply he must feel since even his blood can speak. Similarly, Portia, learning of the penalty that Antonio must pay for defaulting on his debt, tells Salerio, "There are some shrewd contents in yond same paper / That steals the color from Bassanio's cheek" (III, ii, ll. 243-244).

Another important facet of Shakespeare's rhetorical repertoire is his use of allusion. An allusion is a reference to another author or to an historical figure or event. Very often Shakespeare alludes to the heroes and heroines of Ovid's *Metamorphoses*. For example, in Cymbeline an entire room is decorated with images illustrating the stories from this classical work, and the heroine, Imogen, has been reading from this text. Similarly, in *Titus Andronicus* characters not only read directly from the *Metamorphoses*, but a subplot re-enacts one of the *Metamorphoses's* most famous stories, the rape and mutilation of Philomel.

Another way Shakespeare uses allusion is to drop names of mythological, historical, and literary figures. In *The Taming of the Shrew*, for instance, Petruchio compares Katharina, the woman whom he is courting, to Diana (II, i, l. 55), the virgin goddess, in order to suggest that Katharina is a man-hater. At times, Shakespeare will allude to well-known figures without so much as mentioning their names. In *Twelfth Night*, for example, though the Duke and Valentine are ostensibly interested in Olivia, a rich countess, Shakespeare asks his audience to compare the Duke's emotional turmoil to the plight of Acteon, whom the goddess Diana transforms into a deer to be hunted and killed by Acteon's own dogs:

Duke:	That instant was I turn'd into a hart,
	And my desires, like fell and cruel hounds,
	E'er since pursue me.
	[. . .]
Valentine:	But like a cloistress she will veiled walk,
	And water once a day her chamber round . . . .
	(I, i, l. 20 ff.)

Shakespeare's use of puns spotlights his exceptional wit. His comedies in particular are loaded with puns, usually of a sexual nature. Puns work through the ambiguity that results when multiple senses of a word are evoked; homophones often cause this sort of ambiguity. In *Antony and Cleopatra*, Enobarbus believes "there is mettle in death" (I, ii, l. 146), meaning that there is "courage" in death; at the same time, mettle suggests the homophone metal, referring to swords made of metal causing death. In early editions of Shakespeare's work there was no distinction made between the two words. Antony puns on the word "earing," (I, ii, ll. 112-114) meaning both plowing (as in rooting out weeds) and hearing: he angrily sends away a messenger, not wishing to hear the message from his wife, Fulvia: " . . . O then we bring forth weeds,/ when our quick minds lie still, and our ills told us/Is as our earing." If ill-natured news is planted in one's "hearing," it will render an "earing" (harvest) of ill-natured thoughts. A particularly clever pun, also in *Antony and Cleopatra*, stands out after Antony's troops have fought Octavius's men in Egypt: "We have beat him to his camp.

Run one before,/And let the queen know of our gests" (IV, viii, ll. 1-2). Here "gests" means deeds (in this case, deeds of battle); it is also a pun on "guests," as though Octavius' slain soldiers were to be guests when buried in Egypt.

One should note that Elizabethan pronunciation was in several cases different from our own. Thus, modern readers, especially Americans, will miss out on the many puns based on homophones. The textual notes will point out many of these "lost" puns, however.

Shakespeare's sexual innuendoes can be either clever or tedious depending upon the speaker and situation. The modern reader should recall that sexuality in Shakespeare's time was far more complex than in ours and that characters may refer to such things as masturbation and homosexual activity. Textual notes in some editions will point out these puns but rarely explain them. An example of a sexual pun or innuendo can be found in *The Merchant of Venice* when Portia and Nerissa are discussing Portia's past suitors using innuendo to tell of their sexual prowess:

> Portia: I pray thee, overname them, and as thou namest them, I will describe them, and according to my description level at my affection.
>
> Nerissa: First, there is the Neapolitan prince.
>
> Portia: Ay, that's a colt indeed, for he doth nothing but talk of his horse, and he makes it a great appropriation to his own good parts that he can shoe him himself. I am much afeard my lady his mother played false with the smith.
> (I, ii, ll. 35-45)

The "Neapolitan prince" is given a grade of an inexperienced youth when Portia describes him as a "colt." The prince is thought to be inexperienced because he did nothing but "talk of his horse" (a pun for his penis) and his other great attributes. Portia goes on to say that the prince boasted that he could "shoe him [his horse] himself," a possible pun meaning that the prince was very proud that he could masturbate. Finally, Portia makes an attack upon the prince's mother, saying that "my lady his mother played false with the smith," a pun to say his mother must have committed adultery with a blacksmith to give birth to such a vulgar man having an obsession with "shoeing his horse."

It is worth mentioning that Shakespeare gives the reader hints when his characters might be using puns and innuendoes. In *The Merchant of Venice*, Portia's lines are given in prose when she is joking, or engaged in bawdy conversations. Later on the reader will notice that Portia's lines are rhymed in poetry, such as when she is talking in court or to Bassanio. This is Shakespeare's way of letting the reader know when Portia is jesting and when she is serious.

Shakespeare's Dramatic Verse

Finally, the reader will notice that some lines are actually rhymed verse while others are in verse without rhyme; and much of Shakespeare's drama is in prose. Shakespeare usually has his lovers speak in the language of love poetry which uses rhymed couplets. The archetypal example of this comes, of course, from *Romeo and Juliet*:

> The grey-ey'd morn smiles on the frowning night,
> Check'ring the eastern clouds with streaks of light,
> And fleckled darkness like a drunkard reels
> From forth day's path and Titan's fiery wheels.
> (II, iii, ll. 1-4)

Here it is ironic that Friar Lawrence should speak these lines since he is not the one in love. He, therefore, appears buffoonish and out of touch with reality. Shakespeare often has his characters speak in rhymed verse to let the reader know that the character is acting in jest, and vice-versa.

Perhaps the majority of Shakespeare's lines are in blank verse, a form of poetry which does not use rhyme (hence the name blank) but still employs a rhythm native to the English language, iambic pentameter, where every second syllable in a line of ten syllables receives stress. Consider the following verses from *Hamlet*, and note the accents and the lack of end-rhyme:

> The síngle ánd pecúliar lífe is bóund
> With áll the stréngth and ármor óf the mínd
> (III, iii, ll. 12-13)

The final syllable of these verses receives stress and is said to have a hard, or "strong," ending. A soft ending, also said to be "weak," receives no stress. In *The Tempest*, Shakespeare uses a soft ending to shape a verse that demonstrates through both sound (meter) and sense the capacity of the feminine to propagate:

> and thén I lóv'd thee
> And shów'd thee áll the quálitíes o' th' ísle,
> The frésh spríngs, bríne-pits, bárren pláce and fértile.
> (I, ii, ll. 338-40)

The first and third of these lines here have soft endings.

In general, Shakespeare saves blank verse for his characters of noble birth. Therefore, it is significant when his lofty characters speak in prose. Prose holds a special place in Shakespeare's dialogues; he uses it to represent the speech habits of the common people. Not only do lowly servants and common citizens speak in prose, but important, lower class figures also use this fun, at times ribald variety of speech. Though Shakespeare crafts some very ornate lines in verse, his prose can be equally daunting, for some of his characters may speechify and break into double-talk in their attempts to show sophistication. A clever instance of this comes when the Third Citizen in *Coriolanus* refers to the people's paradoxical lack of power when they must elect Coriolanus as their new leader once Coriolanus has orated how he has courageously fought for them in battle:

> We have power in ourselves to do it, but it is a power that we have no power to do; for if he show us his wounds and tell us his deeds, we are to put our tongues into those wounds and speak for them; so, if he tell us his noble deeds, we must also tell him our noble acceptance of them. Ingratitude is monstrous, and for the multitude to be ingrateful were to make a monster of the multitude, of the

which we, being members, should bring ourselves to be
monstrous members.
(II, ii, ll. 3-13)

Notice that this passage contains as many metaphors, hideous
though they be, as any other passage in Shakespeare's dramatic verse.
When reading Shakespeare, paying attention to characters who
suddenly break into rhymed verse, or who slip into prose after
speaking in blank verse, will heighten your awareness of a
character's mood and personal development. For instance, in
Antony and Cleopatra, the famous military leader Marcus Antony
usually speaks in blank verse, but also speaks in fits of prose (II, iii,
ll. 43-46) once his masculinity and authority have been questioned.
Similarly, in *Timon of Athens*, after the wealthy Lord Timon aban-
dons the city of Athens to live in a cave, he harangues anyone whom
he encounters in prose (IV, iii, l. 331 ff.). In contrast, the reader
should wonder why the bestial Caliban in *The Tempest* speaks in
blank verse rather than in prose.

Implied Stage Action

When we read a Shakespearean play, we are reading a performance text. Actors interact through dialogue, but at the same time
these actors cry, gesticulate, throw tantrums, pick up daggers, and
compulsively wash murderous "blood" from their hands. Some of
the action that takes place on stage is explicitly stated in stage directions. However, some of the stage activity is couched within the
dialogue itself. Attentiveness to these cues is important as one con-
ceives how to visualize the action. When Iago in *Othello* feigns concern for Cassio whom he himself has stabbed, he calls to the
surrounding men, "Come, come:/Lend me a light" (V, i, ll. 86-87). It
is almost sure that one of the actors involved will bring him a torch
or lantern. In the same play, Emilia, Desdemona's maidservant, asks
if she should fetch her lady's nightgown and Desdemona replies,
"No, unpin me here" (IV, iii, l. 37). In *Macbeth*, after killing Duncan,
Macbeth brings the murder weapon back with him. When he tells
his wife that he cannot return to the scene and place the daggers to
suggest that the king's guards murdered Duncan, she castigates him:
"Infirm of purpose/Give me the daggers. The sleeping and the dead

are but as pictures" (II, ii, ll. 50-52). As she exits, it is easy to visualize Lady Macbeth grabbing the daggers from her husband.

For 400 years, readers have found it greatly satisfying to work with all aspects of Shakespeare's language—the implied stage action, word choice, sentence structure, and wordplay—until all aspects come to life. Just as seeing a fine performance of a Shakespearean play is exciting, staging the play in one's own mind's eye, and revisiting lines to enrich the sense of the action, will enhance one's appreciation of Shakespeare's extraordinary literary and dramatic achievements.

Historical Background

When Shakespeare began writing plays, the English stage was still in its infancy. Because of strong religious attitudes, for centuries the only types of drama allowed were allegories, such as *Everyman*, which preached moral lessons in a highly formalized fashion. In England, however, things began to change during the early 1500s, under the very secular King Henry VIII. For the first time, plays, such as *Ralph Roister Doister* and *Gammer Gurton's Needle* began showing real people in real-life situations. Still, their plots and characterizations were relatively primitive. It is astonishing to realize that only a few decades later, Shakespeare and his contemporaries would raise staged drama to the heights of artistic excellence and sophistication.

Only a handful of theaters existed in Shakespeare's time, and the one with which he was most associated was the Globe. Circular in shape (a reference by Chorus in *Henry V* calls it "this wooden O"), it had a small stage that protruded onto an open courtyard. In box seats overlooking this space sat the nobles, merchants, and other people of wealth. On the bare earth were the common folk ("groundlings"), who paid a few pennies for admission and stood for the entire performance.

Except for a balcony, a few trapdoors, and tapestry curtains, the Elizabethan stage presented little in the way of theatrical illusion. Nor did the audience demand it. Unlike theatergoers of today, who look for constant action, they were more interested in opulent costumes and long, poetic speeches. They were also accustomed to imagining much of the action, which was typically suggested by the dialogue or conveyed by offstage sound effects. In *Henry V*, for example, whose setting switches from England to France and whose climax is a battle, Shakespeare uses a player called Chorus to "set the scene" in the minds of the audience. This man narrates the story and gives key bits of information, such as the fact that three of Henry's trusted advisors are traitors, and describes vividly large-scale locales, such as the battlefield.

Like Shakespeare's other history dramas, *Henry V* takes a number of liberties with the truth. At the actual Battle of Agincourt, for example, the English army was outmanned 3 to 1—not 5 to 1, as in the play. Nor was the battle the decisive one of the war; in fact, it took Henry three more years to conquer France, and the final conflict occurred at Normandy.

Even more interestingly, Shakespeare willfully ignores the real hero of the battle—the English archer. What won the day in 1415 was the use of a new weapon, the longbow, which could send armor-piercing arrows from a great distance and with deadly accuracy. Each time the heavily encumbered French knights tried to charge, their horses were stopped by long, sharpened stakes that the English had embedded in the earth. As the attack bogged down, the longbowmen instantly rained thousands upon thousands of arrows upon them. The result was a frightful slaughter of the mounted troops, but virtually no British losses. So effective was the longbow, in fact, that it ended the use of an armored cavalry forever.

Shakespeare slights this aspect of the story because his real subject is not the common soldier, but Henry himself. Throughout the play, the focus is on Henry—his heroic exploits, his stirring oratory, even his faults and failings. In the end, we have not only a tapestry of war, but also a portrait of a complex, magnetic, larger-than-life character, the complete Shakespearean hero.

Master List of Characters

Chorus—*A player who introduces the drama, but takes no part in it.*

Henry V—*King of England; newly crowned.*

Duke of Exeter—*Uncle of Henry V; also a soldier and a statesman.*

Duke of Bedford—*Henry's brother.*

Duke of Gloucester—*Henry's younger brother.*

Duke of York—*Henry's cousin.*

Archbishop of Canterbury—*Head of the Catholic church in England; chief religious leader.*

Bishop of Ely—*Assistant to the Archbishop.*

Earl of Cambridge, Lord Scroop, Sir Thomas Grey—*English nobles but traitors to the crown.*

Earl of Westmoreland, Earl of Salisbury, Earl of Warwick—*English nobles.*

Captain Fluellen—*A patriotic Welsh officer in Henry's army while in France.*

Captain Gower—*Another Welsh officer; friend of Fluellen.*

Captain Jamy—*A Scottish officer in Henry's army while in France.*

Captain Macmorris—*An Irish officer in Henry's army while in France.*

Bardolph, Pistol, Nym—*Thieves and cowards; all were friends of Henry during his wild youth.*

Boy—*Young man who at first associates with Bardolph, Pistol, and Nym.*

Hostess Quickly—*Peasant woman; wife of Pistol.*

Michael Williams, John Bates, Alexander Court—*Soldiers in Henry's army.*

Charles VI—*King of France.*

The Dauphin—*Son of Charles VI; heir to the throne.*

Constable of France—*Leader of the French armed forces.*

Duke of Burgundy, Duke of Orleans, Duke of Bourbon—*French nobles and military commanders.*

Montjoy—*Herald; responsible for carrying messages to Henry from the French.*

Rambures and Grandpre—*French nobles and military commanders.*

Duke of Bretagne, Duke of Berri—*French nobles.*

Queen Isabel—*Wife of Charles VI.*

Katharine —*Daughter of Charles VI.*

The Lord Grandpre, The Lord Beaumont—*French noble and military commander.*

Summary of the Play

This play celebrates one of history's most astounding military upsets, the English victory over the French at Agincourt during the Hundred Years' War. Except for a few interludes of comic relief, the action proceeds with no subplots or other complications.

As the play opens in about 1414, the newly crowned Henry is considering waging war on France. His advisors, the leading English nobles and the Archbishop of Canterbury, unanimously urge this action. Canterbury says that France is Henry's by right, as he is descended from a French queen; the Archbishop also knows, however, that the Church's huge property holdings, now threatened by a state takeover, will be safe if France is conquered.

Just as Henry agrees to the war, the French ambassador arrives bearing a package from the French Dauphin. It is a quantity of tennis balls—a deliberate insult to Henry, who in his youth was a carousing playboy. This stiffens the king's determination to "venge" himself on the French.

As England prepares for war, Henry summons three of his advisors. They are, as we know, spies for France. Henry is also aware of their treachery and sends them to their deaths.

The scene shifts to the French court, where King Charles VI's advisors haughtily express their contempt of the English. The French army, they believe, is vastly superior in numbers and equipment and is in no danger from these invaders. Even when word comes that Henry is besieging the town of Harfleur, the Dauphin does not send soldiers to its aid.

At Harfleur, however, the relatively small English army is having trouble taking the town. Inspired by a speech by their valiant warrior king, they finally prevail, but the struggle is costly. Weakened by battle, Henry's troops are now falling ill. With winter approaching, he decides to retreat to the coastal town of Calais.

At this point, the French move against him. Amassing an army that is 60,000 men strong, the French march to the town of Agincourt and prepare for combat. Henry's men number only 12,000, and they are ragged and exhausted. The French camp is more confident than ever.

On the eve of the conflict, Henry assumes a disguise and passes unrecognized among his troops. He learns that despite their physical distress, their patriotism and fighting spirit are still strong. These visits also prompt him to reflect philosophically on his own role—the heavy responsibilities of being a king and its sometimes dubious rewards. But as the new day dawns, he again rises to the occasion, exhorting his troops with another soul-stirring speech. When a French messenger arrives to demand a surrender, his answer is scornful defiance.

The battle begins. From the onstage action, we can see only that the English are fighting fiercely and bravely. Henry is in the thick of it, giving blow for blow. But he, like his men, is so exhausted that when the French messenger arrives again, Henry must ask him who won. Against all odds, the English are victorious! While losing just a few dozen soldiers, the English have massacred nearly 10,000 French—a devastating triumph that seems little short of miraculous.

The play ends on a note of reconciliation, as Henry courts the beautiful Katharine and wins her heart. Soon after, she is given to him in marriage by her father, King Charles VI, as he surrenders his crown. The two countries have resolved their differences at last, and Charles is wise enough to see the peacetime prosperity that lies ahead.

Estimated Reading Time

Allow two hours for the first reading, disregarding textual notes. After that, allow one hour per act for a close, careful reading, note taking, and test preparation.

SECTION TWO

Act I

Scenes 1 and 2

New Characters:

Chorus: *a player who introduces the drama, but takes no part in it*

Archbishop of Canterbury: *head of the Catholic church in England; chief religious leader*

Bishop of Ely: *assistant to the Archbishop*

Henry V: *King of England*

Duke of Exeter: *uncle of Henry V; also a soldier and a statesman*

Duke of Bedford: *a brother of Henry*

Duke of Gloucester: *Henry's younger brother*

Duke of York: *Henry's cousin*

Summary

Chorus begins by delivering a prologue to put the audience in the proper frame of mind. The play's wide scope, he says, cannot be expressed by theatrical means alone. "Can this cock-pit [i.e., the Globe Theater] hold/The vasty fields of France?" He urges the audience to imagine for themselves the effects that cannot be staged—the battle of Agincourt, the prancing of horses, even Shakespeare's distortions of time, "jumping o'er times,/Turning th' accomplishment of many years/Into an hourglass. . . ."

Act I Scene 1 opens with a conversation between the Archbishop of Canterbury and his assistant, the Bishop of Ely. Canterbury is worrying about a bill currently under consideration by Parliament. The bill, brought up by the House of Commons, would have the state strip the Church of its vast property holdings—"the better half of our possession." Only an appeal to the king, who shares power with Parliament, can prevent this tremendous loss.

Canterbury then gives a glowing description of Henry. Although wild and reckless in his youth, Henry has rapidly matured into a wise and able king since the death of his father. Ely agrees.

Canterbury then says that he has begun urging Henry to wage a war of conquest on France, arguing that the French Crown is rightfully his because Henry's great-grandfather had married a French queen. Revealing his true motive, he adds that so rich a prize would make Parliament forget all about seizing the Church's land. The two churchmen exit to join Henry and his chief advisors, who are about to receive an ambassador from France.

Act I Scene 2 finds Henry, Exeter, and Westmoreland preparing for the ambassador's arrival and discussing a possible action against France. Canterbury enters, and Henry asks him to explain, in detail, how he justifies England's claim on the French throne. The archbishop answers by describing a "Salic" (either French or German) law that bars the passing of the Crown through the female side of the family. Henry's great-grandfather, Edward III, had married a French queen, Isabella. The inheritance should have come down through his descendants instead of hers; therefore, Henry should be king of France. Canterbury further supports his case with a long recitation of Henry's family history.

Exeter and Westmoreland, too, speak in favor of war, but Henry is hesitant. He fears that Scotland, a subject state always resentful of the English, will rebel if he takes the army to France. At Canterbury's suggestion, Henry decides to keep three-quarters of the army at home to maintain order in Scotland and to use the remaining quarter abroad. Resolving to "bend [France] to our awe,/Or break it all to pieces," he summons the ambassador.

The ambassador enters bearing a rather unusual gift from his master, the Dauphin—a quantity of tennis balls. Their meaning is clear from the Dauphin's written message. He rejects Henry's claim to "some certain dukedoms" in France and sarcastically adds that "you savour too much of your youth," implying that Henry "should be playing tennis instead of governing."

Stung by this a flagrant insult, Henry threatens to send the tennis balls back as cannonballs. "Tell you the Dauphin I am coming on/To venge me as I may," he warns, vowing to "chide this Dauphin at his father's door."

Analysis

The three issues central to the play that are introduced in Act I are Henry's moral character, the political situation in England, and the relationship between Henry and the Dauphin.

What we learn about Henry's character from the two churchmen is overwhelmingly positive. In fact, lines 23 to 70 are one long string of compliments, beginning "The King is full of grace and sweet regard" and ending ". . . we must needs admit the means/ How things [i.e., Henry] are perfected." He seems to be a perfect king—and indeed, this is one of the dominant themes in the play. The English triumph at Agincourt on St. Crispin's Day was, to Shakespeare's audience, what the Fourth of July is to Americans— an occasion of honor, symbolizing the country's highest ideals. The play is a celebration of both the historical reality and the by-then legendary qualities of Henry. The young king was thought by the Elizabethans to epitomize the chivalric code of honor, and to a great extent the play reflects that attitude. In this act, for example, we see his wisdom in seeking the counsel of elder statesmen, his cool self-possession in the face of the Dauphin's insolence, and his political astuteness in turning that insolence to his advantage when he vows to avenge the honor of the throne. Throughout the ensuing acts we will see similar evidence of his military greatness, his warm humanity, and his other admirable qualities.

The reader should beware, however, of seeing Henry as nothing more than a great man. Shakespeare was far too keen a student of human nature to portray a character in terms only of his virtues (or his vices). Henry is no cardboard saint. As we will see, he is a well-rounded, flesh-and-blood human being, with faults and failings and a high degree of all-too-human complexity. He does what a great king does, and thereby wins our admiration; at the

same time, however, grounds for a healthy skepticism are amply
provided.

The same is no less true of the other major characters. Canterbury, for example, has high moral stature as the leader of the
Church—but should his words automatically be trusted? The archbishop has ample reason for flattering Henry, since he is promot-
ing the idea of war in order to protect the Church's properties.

Moreover, Henry's first speech raises further doubts. When asking Canterbury about the Salic law, he pointedly and at length cautions him against bending the truth. Canterbury's words must be
as "pure," he insists, as a newly baptized soul. Is Henry simply asking for an honest report? Or, in warning Canterbury against
"impawning" him and his kingdom, might he be trying to shift his
own responsibility for the war onto someone else? The question
arises again in Act IV, when Henry has a similar debate with one of
his soldiers.

The political situation in England, too, comes into question
here. During Henry's time (and Shakespeare's as well), England was
not a single, harmoniously unified nation, but rather a confedera-
tion of the mother country and three widely different groups, the
Irish, the Scots, and the Welsh. The same was true in the government, which was divided between the three estates of Parliament—
the Church, the House of Commons, and the House of Lords—and
the Crown. Maintaining control over these frequently opposing
factions was one of the monarch's main tasks, and political unity
rarely lasted long.

In this scene, Canterbury and the others describe Henry as a
strong, universally popular king, but at least two facts indicate just
the opposite. First, a major rift has occurred in Parliament between
the House of Commons and the Church, seriously threatening
England from within. Second, the threat of a Scottish uprising raises
an equally serious threat from without. Note that Henry must split
up his army and take only one-fourth of it to France, lest the Scots
rebel while he is away. Is his throne so weak that he must use three-
quarters of his men to keep the peace? Henry will later be seen as
a gifted unifier of his subjects, but at this point, the issue is much
in doubt.

Notice, too, the relationship established here between Henry
and the Dauphin. ("Dauphin" is simply the title of the oldest le-

gitimate son of a French monarch; in this case, the Dauphin is also the titular head of the country's armed forces.) Shakespeare shows the rivalry between England and France, not by pitting king against king, but by matching the young, untested Henry against a man who is, in certain ways, his counterpart. Both are about the same age, and both are (or were, as in Henry's case) heirs to the crown. A comparison is implied. From the French prince's "gift" and message, we can see that he is haughty, disdainful, and impertinent. Is Henry entirely free from such qualities? Much of this drama is on a personal rather than political level, so we must be alert to clues indicating Henry's inner motives.

One more issue should be raised here as well, though it receives less attention here than in some of the scenes to come. It is the matter of Henry's maturity. The Elizabethans well knew, from legend, lore, and Shakespeare's two *Henry IV* plays, that in his youth Henry (then nicknamed Hal) had lived a life of a reckless dissolution, consorting with thieves and scoundrels in an endless round of drinking, mischief, and debauchery. This lifestyle had persisted almost until the very moment of his coronation. At the death of his father, however, he underwent a virtually miraculous transformation, emerging suddenly as man of surpassing probity, sobriety, wisdom, piety, and good sense—in short, someone as remarkable for his virtue as he had been for his vice.

The discrepancy between his past and his present behavior is perhaps the pivotal issue of the play. In myriad forms, the question is constantly and insistently before us. Is the person we see truly a "new," reformed Henry, or just a clever disguise to hide the "old" Hal? It is a matter we will return to frequently.

Several rhetorical devices are used to enrich the play's meaning. For example, Ely uses the following garden metaphor to recall how Henry once consorted with riffraff but then became a model of kingly sweetness:

> The strawberry grows underneath the nettle,
> And wholesome berries thrive and ripen best
> Neighboured by fruit of base quality.

Also, a simile likens Henry's "contemplation" to "the summer grass," which grows "fastest by night" (alone or unseen). Here, as throughout the play, images from nature are used to symbolize human qualities.

Study Questions

1. Briefly explain why Chorus is used to introduce the play.

2. In Scene 1, what proposed law is worrying the Archbishop of Canterbury, and why?

3. How is Canterbury trying to prevent passage of this law?

4. What do we learn about Henry's personality from Canterbury and Ely?

5. How does Canterbury justify Henry's claim to the French throne?

6. How do Henry's advisors feel about this matter?

7. Why does Henry decide to use only a quarter of his army against France?

8. Who is the Dauphin?

9. What gift does the French ambassador bring to Henry from the Dauphin? What does it imply?

10. What is Henry's reaction to the gift?

Answers

1. Chorus is needed because certain effects, such as battles or distortions of time and place, cannot be staged. Chorus tells the audience to use their imaginations in such cases.

2. Parliament is considering a law allowing the state to seize the Church's properties.

3. He is suggesting that Henry conquer France instead, gaining a much more valuable prize for England and causing Parliament to forget about taking Church lands.

4. We learn that Henry was a wild youth, but is now sober and competent.

5. Canterbury says that under Salic law, the Crown must pass through the male side of the family. Since Henry's great-grandfather married a French queen, Henry is the rightful heir.

6. They favor Canterbury's position and likewise urge war.

7. Henry needs the remainder to keep control over Scotland, a rebellious subject country.

8. The Dauphin is the Prince of France, Charles VI's son.

9. The Dauphin sends tennis balls, implying that Henry is still a playboy and not fit to be a king.

10. He rejects the gift and vows to avenge himself through war.

Suggested Essay Topics

1. What perception of Henry do we see among the English characters? What is their estimation of his character and personality? What different perception do we see among the French? How do these attitudes affect their political decisions?

2. Like any leader embarking on war, Henry needs the power of a united people behind him. What hint do we get that all is not well within England? How would disunity lessen his power against France?

SECTION THREE

Act II

Prologue

Summary

Chorus announces that England is completing preparations for war. Word of this has reached Paris and has caused alarm, and three of Henry's trusted former advisors—the Earl of Cambridge, Lord Scroop, and Sir Thomas Grey—have been bribed to spy on him. The first scene, says Chorus, is set in London, but he says the ensuing scenes will take them to Southampton, where the assembled army is about to depart, and then to France.

Analysis

As before, Chorus' prologue is used to verbally create effects that could not be staged, such as the passage of months during which the army made ready for battle and the geographical shift from London to Southampton to Paris. The speech also condenses an important piece of background information—the espionage of Cambridge, Scroop, and Grey. This allows Shakespeare to dispense with this subplot quickly and to focus attention on Henry's reaction, which reveals much about his character.

Study Questions

1. Do the English people support the war with France?
2. In line 8, is "Expectation" a simile, a metaphor, or a personification?

3.   What is the French attitude toward Henry's invasion?

4.   What simile is used to image England's national spirit?

5.   Who are the three "corrupted men"?

6.   What plan do the three conspirators have?

7.   Where is the first scene located?

8.   Where will the following scene take place?

9.   Where will the last scene in Act II take place?

10. What does Chorus call "a nest of hollow bosoms"?

Answers

1.   Yes. "All the youth of England are on fire" to join the army.

2.   It is a personification.

3.   They "shake in their fear" and wish to "divert the English purposes."

4.   The simile used is "Like little body with a mighty heart," line 17.

5.   They are traitors Cambridge, Scroop, and Grey.

6.   The conspirators' plan is assassination "by their hands this grace of kings must die." (line 28)

7.   It is in London.

8.   It will take place in Southampton.

9.   It will take place in France.

10. He refers to the hearts of the three spies.

Suggested Essay Topics

1.   Write an essay contrasting the imagery used here to describe the English with that used to describe the French, especially as it relates to parts of the human body. What does it imply about the national spirit of each country?

2.   After seeing the arrogance of the Dauphin earlier, how would an audience most likely react to the news that the French

are afraid of the English—and that they have hired assas-
sins to kill Henry? Discuss the characterization of the French
at this point in the play.

Act II, Scene 1

New Characters:

Bardolph, Pistol, Nym: *thieves and cowards; all were friends of
Henry during his wild youth*

Boy: *young man who at first associates with Bardolph, Pistol, and
Nym*

Hostess Quickly: *peasant woman; wife of Pistol*

Summary

In this scene, five low-class characters—Pistol, Bardolph, Nym,
Hostess Quickly, and a boy—meet on a London street. Nym and
Bardolph appear first, and we learn that their friend Pistol has
married Hostess Quickly, who is Nym's former fiancée. When the
couple enters, Nym insults Pistol by calling him "host" instead of
his preferred title, "ancient." This precipitates a quarrel that leads
to a mock duel, as both draw their swords but are too cowardly to
use them.

They are interrupted by the entrance of the boy, who tells
Hostess Quickly that the infamous John Falstaff, the gang's aged
leader, is seriously ill. She exits, and a threat from Bardolph soon
persuades the two men to make up. Pistol ends the scene by saying that he intends to become a profiteer in the coming war.

Analysis

This scene departs from the main action to introduce a small
band of "low," or minor, characters with whom Henry had consorted during his misspent youth. (The titles they go by—corporal, lieutenant, ancient—are fictitious; none of the men is a regular
soldier.) The first three had figured prominently in Shakespeare's
two preceding history plays, *Henry IV, Part I* and *Henry IV, Part II*,
so the audience would be familiar with them already. Here,

however, their relationship with Henry is severed. Pistol alone has dialogue with him, and even then Henry hides behind a disguise. Also, their activities have no discernible effect on him or on the course of events.

One reason for this change is obvious. A king hobnobbing with such lowlifes would be considered altogether inappropriate. Their concerns are wholly different, and none of the gang has anything meaningful to contribute to the state's governance. Shakespeare is not content, however, to dispense with the matter as lightly as that. Hostess Quickly flatly blames Henry for Falstaff's impending death, saying, "The King has killed his heart." This charge would weigh heavily with the Elizabethans, among many of whom "Fat Jack" had attained the status of a folk hero. But even to a modern audience, the accusation injects a sour and pungently personal note, implying that Henry is, at best, aloof and, at worst, perfidious. Once again, his public persona is compromised by his private acts.

If these swaggering, hard-drinking rascals do not impel the play's main action, what functions do they have? One is to provide comic relief, counterbalancing the serious matters of state with their ridiculous brawls and brags. They also serve as foil characters—moral opposites of Henry, Exeter, and the others—and their unprincipled behavior negatively reflects the noble values seen in the court and on the battlefield.

One clue to this theme is the imagery. Pistol addresses the others as "tyke," "Iceland dog," "cur," "egregious dog," and so forth, branding them repeatedly as low, quarrelsome, worthless dogs, whereas Exeter and others will later refer to Henry's "pedigree" and use similarly contrasting images. As is typical in a Shakespeare play, the animalistic personalities of the low characters highlight and intensify the exalted qualities of the king. Also typical, the commoners speak in prose (and frequently incorrect prose, at that), while the nobles use the much more elevated form of blank verse (unrhymed iambic pentameter).

Study Questions

1. What titles do the characters in this scene go by?

2. Are these titles official?

3. What news does the boy bring?

4. Who is Falstaff?

5. Who repeatedly says, "There's the humour of it"?

6. What does "shog off" mean?

7. With what kind of harm do Pistol and Nym threaten each other?

8. Name one kind of recurring animal imagery in this scene.

9. Pistol says he means to be a "sutler ... unto the camp." What is this?

10. Where do the characters go at the end of this scene?

Answers

1. They call themselves "Ancient" Pistol, "Lieutenant" Bard-olph, and "Corporal" Nym.

2. No. None of the three belongs to the army.

3. He says Falstaff is dying.

4. "Sir" John Falstaff was the leader of this gang until he fell ill.

5. This is Nym's refrain.

6. It means "go away."

7. They both draw swords.

8. The metaphor of dogs is repeatedly used.

9. A sutler is a seller of provisions.

10. They go to Falstaff's bedside.

Suggested Essay Topics

1. Describe or exemplify some of the lot characters' comic tech-niques: puns, insults, parody, *non sequiturs, double entendres*, malapropisms. Give at least three or four specific instances from this scene.

2. This scene contains at least five references to various kinds of canines. Identify each of these, define it, and give its meta-phoric meaning as well.

Act II, Scene 2

New Characters:

Earl of Cambridge, Lord Scroop, Sir Thomas Grey: *English nobles, but traitors to the crown*

Earl of Westmoreland: *English noble*

Duke of Bedford: *Henry's brother*

Summary

Now in Southampton, we see Exeter, Bedford, and Westmoreland, Henry's three most trusted advisors, discussing a plot involving three other advisors, the Earl of Cambridge, Lord Scroop, and Sir Thomas Grey, whom the French have paid to spy on Henry. As the scene unfolds, however, we find that the king, too, is suspicious of the conspirators and has prepared writs of impeachment for treason.

Henry soon enters, together with Cambridge, Scroop, and Grey. The king asks their advice in deciding the fate of a man who, while drunk, voiced an insult against him. He says he is inclined to be lenient, but the three unanimously argue the opposite. Henry thereupon hands them each a writ disclosing their plot and exposing them as traitors.

Unmasked, the three admit their wrongs and plead for mercy, but to no avail. Henry says that they, by urging the maximum penalty a moment before, have condemned themselves out of their own mouths:

> The mercy that was quick in us but late
> By your own counsel is suppressed and killed.

By saying "I will weep for thee," he orders them to their death and then returns immediately to his primary concern, preparations for war.

Analysis

This scene illuminates some of the play's most important underlying issues, beginning with that of Henry's character. The standard critical interpretation of *Henry V* says that it is Shakespeare's anthem to the legendary warrior-king of Agincourt, and that Henry himself is a model of the ideal Christian ruler. To such critics, this scene exemplifies his balance of mercy (in pardoning the man who insulted him) and justice (condemning enemies of England), as well as his wisdom in letting the guilty parties decide their own fate.

As mentioned above, however, other critics find Henry's motives less noble, arguing that because he already knows of the plot, he may be simply playing a cat-and-mouse game with the three men in this scene. Rather than forthrightly accusing them, he hands them the papers that lay bare their plot, and then, when they pale at the revelation, he seems to taunt them:

> What see you in those papers, that your lose
> So much complexion?—Why, look you, how they change,
> Their cheeks are paper!

As for the story of the drunken man, skeptics would see more manipulation than wisdom in it, interpreting this contrivance as a means of entrapment.

Henry's admirers also point to the self-control he demonstrates here—an ability to rise above his own feelings when required to do so by his kingly duties. In a highly personal passage he tells the three:

> I will weep for thee;
> For this revolt of thine methinks is like
> Another fall of man.

And at the time of sentencing he forswears a personal motive:

> Touching our person, seek we no revenge,
> But we our kingdom's safety must so tender,
> Whose ruin you [have] sought, that to her laws
> We do deliver you. Get you therefore hence,
> Poor miserable wretches, to your death.

The issue here is a dichotomy between mercy and justice—which in this case means a denial of mercy. To those who see only

goodness in Henry, his judgment shows a steadfast adherence to duty. Though compassionate, he suppresses his own feelings, because as king he must uphold the law, which in time of war requires death for any act of treason.

Again, however, others would disagree, noting how effortlessly Henry slips back and forth between the personal level (referring to himself as "I") and the official level (using the royal "we"). This could be a convenient device for him to claim personal feelings he does not in fact have, while using his office as an excuse for dealing harshly with the men. His insistence that he "seek[s] no revenge" seems to support this, along with his somewhat officious language. Likewise, his frequent religious references give his public pronouncements an air of perhaps false piety. One point is clear enough, however. The existence of three rogue counselors—and note how they balance off the three faithful counselors Exeter, Bedford, and Gloucester—shows yet another fault line in the presumed unity of England.

Turning to rhetorical devices, notice how Henry's dialogue with Scroop and Grey picks up the imagery from Scene 1:

> You must not dare, for shame, to talk of mercy,
> For your own reasons turn into your bosoms
> As dogs upon their masters, worrying you.

Here, a likeness is implied between dogs who attack their own masters and reasons that contradict the reasoner's intentions.

Study Questions

1. Of what crime are Scroop, Grey, and Cambridge guilty?
2. Who knows of the spy plot?
3. What positions do Scroop, Grey, and Cambridge hold?
4. For whom are the three spying?
5. What is their motive?
6. On what decision does Henry seek their advice?
7. What penalty do the three recommend?

8. How do the men discover that their plot has been discovered?

9. What does Henry mean in saying, "Their cheeks are paper"?

10. What sentence does he impose?

Answers

1. They are spies, and are therefore guilty of treason.

2. The truth is known to Henry and his advisors.

3. They, too, are Henry's advisors.

4. They are spying for the French.

5. They are greedy—the French have bought their allegiance.

6. He must decide the sentence for a man convicted of insulting him.

7. They recommend the maximum penalty.

8. Henry hands them papers that tell them so.

9. They have blanched at seeing their plot revealed.

10. He sends them to their death.

Suggested Essay Topics

1. The topic of mercy, and its place in a scheme of justice, is an important theme in the play, arising here and at key moments later. In light of Henry's former friendship with the three spies on the one hand, and his responsibilities as king on the other, write a theme arguing for or against a more merciful verdict on his part. (Consider also the way Henry tests the three men before passing sentence on them.)

2. In Elizabethan thought, treason was considered not only wrong, but fundamentally unnatural, insofar as it upset the ordered state ordained by the Christian God. Find at least three or four references in Henry's accusatory speech, lines 85-151, that support or exemplify this principle. Explain their relevance to the theme.

Act II, Scene 3

Summary

Back in London, outside a tavern, Hostess Quickly tells her husband Pistol that she would like to go with him to the town of Staines, en route to his joining the English army at Southampton. He refuses, saying, "For Falstaff is dead, and we must earn therefore [i.e., grieve for him]." This sets him, Nym, Bardolph, and the boy to reminiscing about their former comrade, with much punning and several bawdy jokes. The short scene ends with Pistol exhorting the others to join him as a camp-follower in France, saying they will make a fortune by living off the misfortune of others.

Analysis

Shakespeare probably inserted this scene as a final farewell to Falstaff, an immensely popular character whom, had he lived, the audience would be expecting to see. No poetry is inspired by his passing, however—a reflection not so much on the author as on these shallow, self-absorbed survivors.

The animal imagery reinforces this impression and, as before, shows the moral state of Pistol, Bardolph, and Nym. ("Nym," incidentally, was Elizabethan slang for pilferer, or thief.) Now their degeneration has progressed beyond dogs to leeches, as Pistol invites the others to join in his parasitic enterprise by saying "Yoke-fellows in arms, let us to France, like horse-leeches, my boys, to suck, to suck, the very blood to suck." The three will indeed exploit the miseries of war through extortion and theft—and more than one will pay for his misdeeds with his life.

Study Questions

1. Who is the Hostess Quickly?

2. Where is Pistol about to go?

3. What are his plans there?

4. What does Hostess Quickly want?

5. Why does Pistol refuse her request?

6. Whom did Falstaff once call "devils incarnate"?

7. According to the boy, where did Falstaff once see a black flea?

8. To what kind of animal does Pistol metaphorically liken himself and the others, once they will all be in France?

9. What did he mean by this?

10. What are the occupations of Pistol, Bardolph, and Nym?

Answers

1. She is Pistol's wife.

2. He is about to leave for Southampton.

3. He plans to follow the army to France, in an attempt to make money.

4. She wants to go with Pistol to the town of Staines.

5. Pistol is in mourning for the recently deceased Falstaff.

6. He said this about women.

7. He espied it in on Bardolph's nose.

8. He likens himself and the others to horse-leeches.

9. He meant that they would live like parasites, sucking blood (money) from the soldiers.

10. They are thieves, scam artists, and all-around scoundrels.

Suggested Essay Topic

1. Carefully reread Hostess Quickly's dialogue. What is her attitude toward Falstaff? Is it the same as that of the men, or different? How would you compare or contrast her with them? Write an essay analyzing her characterization and its relationship to that of the others.

Act II, Scene 4

New Characters:

Charles VI: *King of France*

The Dauphin: *son of Charles VI; heir to the throne*

Constable of France: *leader of the French armed forces*

Duke of Burgundy, Duke of Orleans, Duke of Bourbon: *French nobles and military commanders*

Summary

The scene now shifts to the French court, where King Charles VI is conferring with his advisors and his son the Dauphin about the English invasion. The king, recalling England's victories over the French at Crecy (1346) and Poitiers (1356) just a few decades earlier, calls for speedy mobilization of the army "To line and new-repair our towns of war/With men of courage and with means defendant."

The Dauphin acknowledges the prudence of his father's words on general principle, saying it is always a good idea to take precautions. He minimizes the present threat, however, by observing that the English throne is "so fantastically borne" that no one need fear the "vain, giddy, shallow, humorous" Henry. For this he is chided by the Constable of France, who points to England's traditional resoluteness and warns against overconfidence.

Here Exeter enters with a warning of his own. Invoking the English victor at Crecy, Henry's ancestor Edward III, Exeter tells Charles to "resign/Your crown and kingdom, indirectly held/From him, the native and true challenger." Henry is coming, he says, "in thunder and in earthquake like a Jove." Exeter also conveys Henry's "scorn and defiance, slight regard [and] contempt" for the Dauphin. The king ends the scene by saying that Henry will receive his answer on the morrow.

Analysis

Here, in a scene that matches the counseling of Henry in Scene 2, Shakespeare contrasts the firmness and unity of the English court

with the divided, somewhat vacillating mood of the French. The Constable's quarrel with the Dauphin betrays some basic disagreements between the country's rulers, and the king's hesitant reaction to Exeter is the opposite of Henry's stinging reply to the Dauphin's messenger.

Also worth noting is the character of the Dauphin, who, like the conspirators in the preceding scene, condemns himself with his own words, "vain, giddy, shallow, humorous." Here, as elsewhere, his similarities to Henry in age and position serve to heighten their differences in personality and temperament. The two are mirror twins. Where Henry in many ways personifies the noblest values of the English, the Dauphin personifies his society's worst failings. The Dauphin's counsel to his father that "Self-love . . . is not so vile a sin/As self-neglecting," for example, is really a way of excusing his own egotistical self-indulgence.

As in previous scenes, metaphors from the animal kingdom are used. The Dauphin calls the English "coward dogs," and Exeter refers to Henry's royal lineage as his "pedigree." Here Shakespeare also includes another kind of imagery, that of garden plants, which was first used by the Bishop of Ely and which will also develop in future scenes. The Constable, for example, says that during his youth, Henry, like the redoubtable Roman Brutus, hid his "constant resolution" under a show of vanity, "as gardeners do with ordure hide those roots/That shall first spring and be most delicate." Soon thereafter, Exeter, referring to Henry's descent from Edward III, calls him "a stem/Of that victorious stock." The metaphoric use of cultivated plants to represent the orderly, controlled, and therefore good world of nature—and by contrast the disorderly, unnatural growth of weeds, representing evil—is a pervasive theme in Shakespeare and does much to enrich the meaning of the play.

Study Questions

1. Who is the Dauphin?

2. What military order does the French king give?

3. What is the Dauphin's opinion of Henry V?

4. How does the Constable of France's opinion compare with the Dauphin's?

5. Who was "the Black Prince of Wales"?

6. What importance did Edward III have in French history?

7. What command does Exeter bring to the French king?

8. What message does Exeter bring to the Dauphin?

9. What threat does Exeter make?

10. What is Charles' response to Exeter?

Answers

1. The Dauphin is the son of the French king and heir to the throne.

2. He orders that the country mobilize for war to defend against the English.

3. He dismissively calls him "vain, giddy, shallow, humorous."

4. The Constable takes the English threat more seriously than the Dauphin does.

5. He was Edward III, Henry V's great-uncle.

6. He defeated the French at the Battle of Crecy a few decades earlier.

7. Exeter commands, in Henry's name, that Charles resign his throne.

8. He rebukes the Dauphin for his insulting gift of tennis balls and expresses Henry's contempt for him.

9. Unless Charles VI resigns, Henry will ravage France like an earthquake.

10. He says he will give Henry his answer on the following day.

Suggested Essay Topics

1. Discuss the pervasive irony in Shakespeare's portrayal of the Dauphin. Focus on the Dauphin's dialogue and its relation to his own manners, morals, attitude, and leadership—especially his decision not to defend Harfleur (see Act III). Also comment on how this irony generalizes to his fellow nobles and ultimately to the French people as a whole.

2. Does Charles VI's estimate of Henry concur with that of this advisors? Do his military orders follow or countermand theirs? Compare or contrast his leadership and personality with Henry's. Include a comment on his response to Exeter in this scene.

Act III

Prologue

Summary

Chorus again calls on the audience to imagine offstage events. Henry has sailed to France and has begun a siege of the town of Harfleur. Meanwhile, a French ambassador tells Henry that the French king is offering Princess Katharine in marriage, along with "some petty and unprofitable dukedoms," if he will end his campaign. Henry rejects this attempt at appeasement.

Analysis

As in all the Prologues, Chorus' diction is elevated and grandiose. The shore is the "rivage," the sea is "inconstant billows," strength is "pith and puissance," the cannons have "fatal mouths," and so forth. Through this rhetoric, Chorus gives an epic, larger-than-life scale to the drama, overcoming the theater's limitations and conferring a mythical importance on the action.

A few details are notable for their apparent inaccuracy. One is the passage describing the helplessness of England, which Chorus says is defended by "grandsires, babies, and old women"—contradicting the fact, mentioned earlier, that three-fourths of the army is still there. Shakespeare may be reminding the audience that despite its military power, the English throne is still somewhat precarious because of the ethnic divisions within the country. As we know, a possible revolt by the Scots, along with the chronic restiveness of the Irish and the Welsh, needs constant attention. This aspect is developed further during Act III.

A second apparent inaccuracy is a reference to the army as "culled and choice-drawn cavaliers." This may be another rhetorical flourish, as, historically speaking, Henry had relatively few such warriors. Most of his army was made up of infantry, or footsoldiers, who were unarmored and carried only swords and longbows.

Study Questions

1. According to Chorus, how fast does this scene fly?
2. What is the "hempen tackle" on which boys climb?
3. What is the course of the voyage that Chorus describes?
4. Who is guarding England in Henry's absence?
5. What are "fatal mouths"?
6. What offer has Henry received from the French king?
7. What is Henry's answer?
8. What sound effects are used here?
9. Where will the present action take place?
10. What is the English army doing there?

Answers

1. It flies "as fast as thought."
2. It is the ship's rigging—ropes and stays.
3. It is from Southampton, England, to Harfleur, France.
4. The country is "guarded with grandsires, babies, and old women."
5. This is a metaphor (metonymy) for cannon muzzles.
6. The king has offered him his daughter Katharine, along with some dukedoms.
7. He refuses.
8. Cannon fire is heard from offstage.
9. It will occur in the French town of Harfleur.
10. It is laying siege to the town.

Suggested Essay Topics

1. Copy the Prologue and make notations as if you were going to recite it. Underline key words or passages, show where pauses should go, and include prompts where there should be special emphasis or feeling. Be prepared to perform it for the class.

2. What examples of words, phrases, or figures of speech can you find that expand the scope of the action to an epic scale? How might these lend a sense of grandeur to the play? Write an essay giving at least three or four specific examples.

Act III, Scene 1

New Character:

Soldiers: *infantrymen in the English army*

Summary

Standing before a gap in the wall surrounding Harfleur, Henry delivers a rallying speech to his troops. Pleading for one more mighty effort, he tells them to cast off their civilized manners and "imitate the action of the tiger." He appeals to their nationalism ("On, on, you [noblest] English"), linking his own leadership with the men's patriotic and religious fervor:

Cry "God for Harry, England, and Saint George!"

Analysis

Henry's oratory here is dazzling. "Once more unto the breach" is among the most famous battle cries in literature, and his injunction to "disguise fair nature with hard-favored rage" masterfully summons the troops' fighting spirit. Imagistically, Henry's soldiers become human instruments of war, their eyes "like the brass cannon." He skillfully uses the men's social status to engender competition between the gentlemen and the yeomen, challenging the former to "be copy now to men of grosser blood/And teach them how to war." The "good yeomen" he likens to leashed greyhounds impatient to be loosed upon the prey. [This may have been Shakespeare's nod to historical truth, for the yeoman-archer was indeed the mainstay of the army during this campaign.]

While there is no denying the rhetorical power of this speech, a closer look reveals certain disquieting elements. Its beginning, for example—"Once more . . . once more"—indicates that the army has already tried to storm the town but has failed. In fact, this charge fails yet again, as we learn in Scene 3.

Likewise, some less-than-noble sentiments may underlie the fine words. Henry tells his men to fight like tigers, which in the modern world would imply ferocity coupled with a degree of grandeur. In the Elizabethan scheme of things, however, the meaning would be somewhat different. The lion, not the tiger, was considered the king of beasts and was ascribed such high qualities as nobility and courage, especially in warfare. (This is why, for example, the lion is used as the national symbol of England.) Yet Henry sidesteps this conventional appeal for a more equivocal one. By invoking the tiger he may be appealing to the soldiers' baser instincts—their animalistic natures—rather than their more heroic, manly natures. In the heat of battle, is he calling for bloodlust instead of bravery?

Moreover, Henry verges on insinuation, rather than inspiration, when he in effect questions the men's parentage: "Dishonor not your mothers" and "attest/That those whom you called father did beget you." This may well be a veiled appeal to guilt instead of valor, and it is buttressed by a challenge to "swear/That you are worth your breeding." Note, too, Henry's simile when he says that the men's fathers were "like so many Alexanders" (i.e., Alexander the Great).

Study Questions

1. What is a siege?

2. To what "breach" does Henry refer?

3. What, says Henry, should they do if not storm the breach?

4. What clue do we get here about the power of the English army?

5. Whom does Henry liken to "so many Alexanders"?

6. What are considered manly virtues during peacetime?

7. What does the simile "like the brass cannon" refer to?

8. Whom are the "noblest English" to set an example for?

9. Who are yeomen?

10. What does the metaphor "the game's afoot" mean?

Answers

1. It is a military attempt to capture a fortified (and usually walled) town.

2. He refers to a gap in the wall surrounding Harfleur.

3. They should "close up the wall with our English dead!"

4. They are not invincible. This is not their first attempt to enter the breach.

5. He alludes to the fathers of his soldiers.

6. Modesty and humility are such virtues.

7. It refers to the eyes of the soldiers.

8. They are to set an example for "those of grosser blood," i.e., the lower classes.

9. Yeomen are free subjects who are commoners, farmers, etc.

10. It means the quarry has been set loose—the hunt has begun.

Suggested Essay Topics

1. Imagine you are a newspaper reporter covering the siege of Harfleur and must describe Henry's speech and his men's reactions to it. In a narrative essay, write a line-by-line paraphrase of the speech, but from time to time interpose responses indicating whether the English troops are inspired, discouraged, skeptical, etc.

2. The class divisions in English society were frequently a source of conflict within the ranks of the army. Discuss the ways in which Henry tries to overcome these in his speech. How might he be exploiting their social differences by stimulating a healthy competition against the enemy? How would this be advantageous militarily? Does he imply that war makes all soldiers equals?

Act III, Scene 2

New Characters:

Captain Fluellen: *a patriotic Welsh officer in Henry's army*

Captain Gower: *another Welsh officer, friend of Fluellen*

Captain Jamy: *a Scottish officer in Henry's army*

Captain Macmorris: *an Irish officer in Henry's army*

Summary

The boy and his friends Pistol, Bardolph, and Nym retreat from the battle, but Fluellen, a Welsh officer, commands them to return to the fray. After the others depart, the boy reflects on the low morals of his companions and decides to part company with them.

Fluellen reenters and is urged by Gower, a fellow Welshman, to help two other officers dig tunnels under the Harfleur wall. They are soon joined by these others—captains Macmorris, an Irishman, and Jamy, a Scot. An argument erupts between Fluellen and Macmorris and is about to escalate into a duel when word arrives that Henry has called a parley of his officers. The two vow to resume their dispute later.

Analysis

This scene begins with an obvious parody of the preceding one, as the ignoble Pistol echoes Henry's speech: "On, on, on, on, on! To the breach, to the breach!" It momentarily breaks the serious mood of the play until Fluellen chases the three rascals back to the battlefront.

Then, however, the boy's soliloquy sounds an interesting new note, as he comments quite explicitly on these rascals. Bardolph is a cowardly ("white-livered") faker, who "faces it out but fights not"; Pistol is likewise all talk and no action, with "a killing tongue and a quiet sword"; and Nym "never broke any man's head but his own, and that was against a post when he was drunk." Recognizing them for the thieves and rogues they are, the boy concludes that "Their villainy goes against my weak stomach, and therefore I must cast it up."

In separating himself from the others, the boy takes on a new stature, emerging as a person of importance and moral authority. Note, too, how closely his deserting of the three rogues mirrors Henry's renunciation of them, implying a parallel between the young man and the king. This will lend significance to the boy's fate in Act IV.

The quarrel between Fluellen and Macmorris, a drama-within-the-drama, underscores the ethnic rivalries that exist just below the surface and recalls the disunity back in England. Shakespeare's audience knew, of course, what the outcome of the play would be, because the Battle of Agincourt was part of every schoolchild's education. He was probably alluding more to contemporary events than to history. Only a year before the play opened in 1600, the English had brutally quelled a major rebellion in Ireland. Such stresses were a constant feature of English life, not unlike the racial tensions sometimes depicted among soldiers in American war movies.

This issue of disunity impels another of Henry's most important characteristics—that of the great unifier. Throughout the play, he will face not only the threat of the French, but also the problem of maintaining peace and harmony among his soldiers. As we see here and will see frequently in the subsequent acts, the domestic quarrels that forced him to divide the army in Act I will constantly be erupting within the ranks. As you read, watch for instances of these divisions, and notice particularly how Henry deals with them in moments of crisis. Much of his stature is derived from his ability to reconcile the various ethnic groups and social classes by personal example, persuasive speechmaking, and sheer force of personality.

Study Questions

1. What action did the French king take between Acts II and III?

2. What does Henry mean by "Once more unto the breach"?

3. What reaction does he get from Pistol, Bardolph, Nym, and the boy?

4. Why do they finally rejoin the battle?

5. What change comes over the boy?

6. What are the "mines" to which Fluellen alludes?

7. Of what nationality are Fluellen, Macmorris, and Jamy?

8. How is this fact important to the situation?

9. What is their personal relationship?

10. Are all their differences resolved in this scene?

Answers

1. He offered Henry a bribe—Princess Katharine and some French dukedoms—to withdraw.

2. He is urging his soldiers to storm Harfleur through a gap in the town's wall.

3. They run the opposite way.

4. Fluellen forcibly turns them around.

5. He recognizes the worthlessness of his companions and decides to leave them.

6. These are holes dug under the wall that are meant to collapse it (a process called "undermining").

7. They are, respectively, Welsh, Irish, and Scottish.

8. Back in England, all three nations are at odds with the ruling English government.

9. They are mutually quarrelsome and disputatious.

10. No. Fluellen and Macmorris plan to continue their fight at a later time.

Suggested Essay Topics

1. This scene enacts roughly the same event as does Act III, Scene 1, but from a different point of view. How might it be considered a "companion piece" to the previous scene—i.e., one that contains enough similarity to suggest a parallel but also important differences? Compare and contrast Henry's noble rhetoric with the attitudes of these "low" characters and that of his one-time boon companion Falstaff.

2. Describe the personalities of Fluellen, Jamy, and Macmorris. To what extent do they seem to be simply caricatures or stereotypes? Which of them is most fully developed in his own right? What do their ethnic rivalries imply about domestic tranquility back in England?

Act III, Scene 3

Summary

At the gates of Harfleur, Henry addresses the French governor with an ultimatum—either surrender the town or see it buried in its own ashes. Henry says his soldiers will "mow like grass" the young girls and children of the town, rape its "pure maidens," seize its "shrill-shrieking daughters," smash the heads of its fathers, and impale "naked infants" on pikes while their mothers run mad with grief. The governor admits that the town has been abandoned by the Dauphin, who was "not ready/To raise so great a siege." Faced with these dire consequences, the governor gives in.

As his army advances to claim the town, Henry, observing that "winter is coming on and sickness growing/Upon our soldiers," decides to "retire to Calais."

Analysis

Once again, we see Henry's oratorical brilliance, in a speech that seems to break the will of the French even when his army could not overcome them physically. We also see his outstanding qualities of leadership. Just as he earlier renounced the French king's offer of a bribe, he here forswears negotiation, in effect saying "Surrender or die." This is the kind of resolute, decisive performance his troops expect—one of the "disciplines of war," in the Elizabethan sense—and Henry rises admirably to the occasion.

While the words are stirring, however, the action here is almost anticlimactic compared with Scene 1, for the victory is gained not by battle, but by threat. Given the other liberties he took with history, Shakespeare might have staged a mighty struggle before the town's capitulation—but he does just the opposite, making the

triumph look almost like a defeat. Far from exulting in his military superiority or marching regally into the town, Henry ends the scene emphasizing his disadvantages, sickness in the ranks, the onset of winter, and the general exhaustion of his soldiers. Through this strategy, the playwright shrewdly heightens the drama of the next act, where the play's real climax occurs.

Some critics raise questions about Henry's speech, which takes up most of the scene. Rather than threatening the town with military harm, he seems badgering and bullying. His horrific details of rape and savagery are at odds with the honorable, principled conduct he claims for himself, and in fact demands from his men soon afterward. Here, again, is the hint of a cruel, sadistic side in Henry that may be masked by his exceptionally virtuous behavior at other times.

Study Questions

1. Why don't the English simply storm the breach and take Harfleur?

2. Is Henry discouraged about their prospects at the start of this scene?

3. In speaking to the men of Harfleur, does Henry accept responsibility for the acts of his soldiers if the town falls?

4. Why does the governor finally surrender?

5. Does Henry make good on his threat to ravage the town?

6. At this point in the play, how powerful does the English army look?

7. What physical disadvantages does Henry's army face?

8. What does the Dauphin's decision about Harfleur tell us about his character?

9. How do the English react to the surrender?

10. Judging from this incident, how do Henry's prospects against the French army look?

Answers

1. They are not militarily strong enough to do so.

2. No, he is resolved to take the town at any cost.

3. No, he says "you yourselves [i.e., the French] are the cause."

4. He says the Dauphin has decided not to send troops to defend the town.

5. No, he tells Exeter, "Use mercy to them all for us, dear uncle."

6. They seem relatively weak and unable to capture the town by force of arms.

7. Winter is approaching and the soldiers are falling ill.

8. It suggests that he is an unreliable leader and a poor supporter of his people.

9. They seem relieved, but not overjoyed.

10. He seems too weak to defeat them.

Suggested Essay Topics

1. What evidence can you cite that Henry uses bluff and bluster, as well as genuine military might, to achieve his ends? Consider his actual accomplishments thus far at Harfleur, his speech to the men of the town, and his command once the victory is in hand.

2. Arguably, the English did not truly win at Harfleur—the French simply lost. Discuss this proposition, with reference to the Dauphin's conduct and to the implications it contains about the French national character and the ensuing events of the play.

Act III, Scene 4

New Character:

Katharine: *daughter of Charles VI*

Summary

In a room of the French palace, we find Princess Katharine getting an English lesson from her serving-woman, Alice. As Alice asks the English words for various parts of the body, the young woman laughs and speaks disparagingly of the language.

Analysis

This scene—more accurately, an interlude—introduces the princess whom Henry will later woo and marry. Though the reason for her interest in learning English is not clearly established, we may assume that Katharine knows her father has offered her to the English king (i.e., as a payoff for leaving France), and she wants to prepare for this.

Here we get a sense of the young woman's lively intelligence, her cheerfulness, and her apparent willingness to go with Henry if necessary. This is important for us to know, because in a purely technical sense, she is little more than a pawn of history, with no choice over her fate. Seeing her as a flesh-and-blood individual makes us care about her. The scene also prepares us for the later action, in which Henry, rather than simply claiming her as a prize of war, is at pains to win her heart. Here we see what he finds attractive about her.

Study Questions

1. Approximately how old is Katharine?

2. Why would she want to learn English?

3. Is she worried or apprehensive about the possibility of marrying Henry?

4. What is her opinion of English?

5. Why are words like "the," "nails," and "elbow" misspelled?

6. Who is Alice?

7. What is the subject of the English lesson?

8. What is "de nick"?

9. What is the likely purpose of such mispronunciations?

10. How would an actor communicate the meaning of French words to an English audience?

Answers

1. She is about 14 or 15.

2. She knows her father has promised her in marriage to Henry.

3. No, she seems light-hearted in this scene.

4. She evidently thinks it is a strange language and very inferior to the French language.

5. Shakespeare spells them phonetically, to reflect the speakers' accents.

6. She is an elderly gentlewoman, Katharine's handmaid.

7. It is about parts of the body.

8. This means "the neck."

9. They are intended to be humorous and to show the princess' easygoing personality.

10. She would use gestures to convey the meaning.

Suggested Essay Topics

1. The emotional tone of this scene is ambiguous, in that it is not always clear whether we should be laughing with the princess or at her. Imagine that you are a theatrical director coaching an actress in this part. Tell how she should recite at least three or four key passages so as to convey the point of view you have chosen. Add stage directions or actions to help clarify the perspective for the audience.

2. The English audience knew the history of Agincourt before seeing this play. In light of this, how does Shakespeare use this scene to anticipate a happy ending? Is it necessary to know anything more about Katharine than we learn in this scene? Why or why not?

Act III, Scene 5

Summary

Elsewhere in the palace, the French king and his advisors discuss, amid some embarrassment, Henry's victory at Harfleur and debate the relative strength of the two warring armies. Charles orders the mobilization of his forces, with which he intends to cut off the English retreat to Calais.

Because it seems clear that the English are not only fatigued and falling ill but are also hopelessly out-numbered, the French king also decides to offer Henry a way out. He sends a herald to demand a ransom, promising in return to spare his army from annihilation.

Analysis

This short scene tells us something more about the temperament of the French king. Unlike his frivolous son and complacent advisors, Charles has sense enough to avoid a fight with the English if he can and spare his country a potentially disastrous defeat. The demand for a ransom is both prudent and appropriate, given the enormous disparity in size between the two armies. In later refusing it, Henry again shows his boldness and tenacity. (Note that this is the second time Henry is tempted to avoid a fight.)

The scene also anticipates the consequences of a French defeat. A loss would engender scorn in the populace—and specifically among French women, who, complains the Dauphin, already "mock at us and plainly say/Our mettle is bred out." In a pointed insult to these overconfident men, the women say "they will give/Their bodies to the lust of English youth/To new-store France with bastard warriors."

Shakespeare inserts this action here because it would otherwise be unstageable, as it would seem anticlimactic to show France after the Battle of Agincourt. This arrangement enables the play to move swiftly from the battle itself to the victorious aftermath in the English camp.

Here, as elsewhere, the French are portrayed as lustful and lazy, in contrast to the spartan English. The contrast is intensified in a

speech by the Constable (lines 15-27) where images of heat and cold reflect the respective qualities of the French and the English. Likewise, the Dauphin takes up the gardening metaphor earlier used by Henry, but applies it to his own people. With evident shame, he asks whether "a few sprays [twigs] of us . . ./Spurt up so suddenly into the clouds/And overlook their grafters?" Should we, he says, be such upstarts as to look down on our own, heroic ancestors? The answer is equally obvious and unflattering.

Study Questions

1. To what news are the French nobles reacting in this scene?

2. What effect has this news had on the French people?

3. How would you describe the mood of the characters here?

4. Whose criticism do the men feel most keenly?

5. What prompts the king to demand for a ransom from Henry?

6. What is the gist of the Constable's speech (lines 15-27)?

7. What opposite images are used here for France and England?

8. What course of action does the Constable urge?

9. Does the French king take this advice?

10. What prediction does the Constable make?

Answers

1. They have learned of Henry's victory at Harfleur.

2. It has substantially lowered their opinion of the army.

3. They are embarrassed, yet still disdainful of the English.

4. They are stung by the insults of their "madams"—wives and girlfriends—who accuse them of cowardice and unmanliness.

5. He believes the English do not stand a chance against his army.

6. He wonders how the cold climate of England could produce such hot-blooded warriors.

7. Heat and cold are used, respectively.

8. He urges an immediate attack on Henry.

9. No, he sends a ransom offer instead.

10. He says that the English will see the mighty French army and, out of fear, pay the ransom.

Suggested Essay Topics

1. What does the French women's "mock" imply about the characters and values of the French men? How might it define the French national character as a whole—and how does this definition compare or contrast with English standards of valor and manliness? Note especially Exeter's speech about the deaths of York and Suffolk (Act IV, Scene 6), in which the devotion of soldier to soldier is held up as the highest possible expression of human love.

2. Analyze the Constable's speech beginning with *"Dieu de batailles."* How are figures of speech used to enlarge his meaning? Might these words betray an underlying uneasiness in him, which he tries to cover with an arrogant facade?

Act III, Scene 6

Summary

Back among the English at Picardy, captains Gower and Fluellen discuss the bravery of Exeter, who has just won an important military skirmish by holding a key bridge further up the river. (This event is not described in detail in the play. Exeter's stand took place in an area called Teroune. Henry and his men needed a nearby river crossing to avoid an exhausting, 50-mile trek to the next bridge. Exeter, while reconnoitering, came upon a small bridge that the French were about to destroy. He drove off the enemy and held out until Henry and his troops arrived.)

Describing the scene in his slow-witted fashion, Fluellen praises both Exeter and another soldier he saw on the bridge, the "Aunchient Pistol." (The Welshman's dialogue, like that of the other

ethnics, Macmorris and Jamy, is sprinkled with idiomatic mispronunciations.) At this point, Pistol himself enters and tries to inter-
cede on behalf of Bardolph, who has been caught stealing and is
under the sentence of death. When Fluellen rejects the plea, Pistol
exits.

Gower then recollects an earlier meeting with Pistol and ex-
poses him as an "arrant counterfeit rascal," though Fluellen remains unconvinced. They are interrupted by the arrival of Henry,
along with Gloucester and some common soldiers. Fluellen relates
the sentence imposed on Bardolph, pointing out that so far the
English have not lost a single man in battle—this thief would be
the first. Nevertheless, Henry upholds the judgment, adding, "We
would have all such offenders cut off." He repeats his order against
looting or committing any other incivility toward French civilians.

At this point, the French herald Montjoy appears, bearing the
French king's demand for ransom. Though admitting that "My army
[is] but a weak and sickly guard," Henry rejects the order out of
hand, in effect making himself the ransom price. Come and get
me, he tells Charles through his messenger: "We would not seek a
battle as we are,/Nor, as we are, we say we will not shun it." To his
own men he says, "We are in God's hand, not theirs."

Analysis

Much has been made about Henry's decision not to pardon
Bardolph, his former companion, for what might be construed as
a petty offense—the theft of a "pyx" from a local church. This object was indeed of relatively little value, being a *paten,* or communion plate rather than a chalice or other golden artifact. However,
the principle involved was an extremely serious one, because by
law any theft from a church was a capital crime. Pardoning
Bardolph would set a momentous precedent, even if Henry were
inclined to do so out of fellow-feeling for an old chum. Here again,
as in the sentencing of the three traitors at Southampton, he must
choose between friendship and duty. Again, he is firm and decisive.

One critic has observed that Bardolph's crime, theft from a
church, is reminiscent of an earlier and much larger "crime," the
bill proposed by the House of Commons to seize all land held by

the Catholic church. If so, Henry's comment, "We would have all such offenders cut off," takes on additional significance, showing his piety and righteousness.

His refusal to pardon Bardolph, however, is not entirely without ambiguity. Is he simply fulfilling the dictates of his office as king, or does this show a basic coldness or insensitivity in him? In the same breath as his seeming denial of Bardolph, Henry announces a strict, somewhat moralistic set of rules, forbidding his soldiers even to use "disdainful language" against the French citizenry. Nobility or hypocrisy? A possible clue appears in Gower's earlier speech describing Pistol as someone who "goes to the wars . . . under the form of a soldier." Speaking generically about "such fellows," Gower goes on at some length about the discrepancy between appearance and reality—underscoring a theme that might apply to Henry himself.

Study Questions

1. Of what two characters does Fluellen speak admiringly? Why?

2. In military terms, what was the effect of Exeter's accomplishment?

3. Does Fluellen seem to be a good judge of character? How do you know?

4. How does Pistol explain Bardolph being sentenced to death for theft?

5. What object did Bardolph steal, and where did he get it?

6. Is the death sentence unduly harsh for such a crime?

7. What is surprising about Henry's refusal to pardon Bardolph?

8. Henry tells the messenger, Montjoy, that his army is sick and enfeebled. What might be his reason for admitting this?

9. Does Henry challenge Charles to a battle?

10. How many losses have the English suffered thus far?

Answers

1. He praises Exeter and Pistol for having taken a militarily important bridge.

2. He saved the army from having to march 50 miles to the next bridge.

3. No, he misjudges Pistol completely.

4. No, he blames it on the goddess Fortune, rather than actual guilt.

5. He stole a "pyx," or communion plate, from a church.

6. No. Under the law of the time, any theft from a church, no matter how minor, was punishable by death.

7. He and Bardolph were friends during their younger days.

8. He might want to lull King Charles into a false sense of security.

9. No, but he says they will not avoid a fight.

10. None. Bardolph will be the first.

Suggested Essay Topics

1. Reread what Pistol says about Bardolph being "Fortune's foe" and the description of Pistol by Gower. How does Pistol's attitude justify the low opinion that the Welshman has formed of him? What does it imply about Pistol's sense of morality? Would Pistol's defense of Bardolph tend to increase or decrease our sympathy for the convicted thief?

2. Shakespeare might have focused this scene on Exeter's defense of the bridge at Teroune—a far more exciting event than the one enacted here. Why, in terms of the play's structure, would that have been a bad idea? What issues might have been lost or overlooked, and how might it have upset the overall momentum of the action?

Act III, Scene 7

New Characters:
Lord Rambures: *a French noble and military commander*
Duke of Orleans: *a French noble and military commander*

Summary

The final scene of this act shifts the focus once again to the French military leaders—the Constable, the Dauphin, Lord Rambures, and others—who are camped opposite Henry at Agincourt and evidently prepared for battle. They spend much of the scene in light-hearted banter. The Dauphin speaks about his own steed, which "bounds from the earth," a Pegasus which "trots the air," and so forth. Orleans tries to cut him short, first remarking that the horse is "the color of nutmeg," and then pleading, "No more, cousin." The other officers join in with punning, bawdy remarks that mock the prince and his "brags." After the Dauphin exits, the Constable sarcastically ridicules his fighting ability.

When the messenger brings news that the English army has encamped "within fifteen hundred paces," the subject turns to Henry. "What a wretched and peevish fellow is this King of England to mope with his fat-brained followers so far out of his knowledge," observes Orleans. The Constable replies that if the English had any sense, "they would run away." To general agreement, Orleans ends the scene and the act with the following supremely confident prediction:

> It is now two o'clock. But, let me see, by ten
> We shall have each a hundred Englishmen.

Analysis

Shakespeare uses this scene to reinforce our impressions of the French before shifting the focus again to the English for most of the climactic Act IV. Once again, we see the vain, egotistical Dauphin swept up in his own importance and indulging in giddy fantasies. And again, we see disunity amongst the officers, as the others register scorn for him—king's son or not. But despite their towering overconfidence, a note of disunity is sounded when Lord Rambures, symbolically referring to English mastiffs, cautions, "That island of England breeds very valiant creatures." Naturally his warning is ignored.

Certainly, the Frenchmen have grounds for confidence, given the support of the people and their own overwhelming military superiority. Yet they come off not as larger than life, but smaller. We see their essential triviality, as they spend the eve of battle preparing for a life-and-death struggle by playing word games. Shakespeare is suggesting that the impending battle is more than a political contest between warring ideologies, or a moral conflict between right and wrong. It is also a test of national character, especially as embodied by Henry and the Dauphin. With the Dauphin at center stage here, the contrast is brought to its highest pitch. Compare his vaporous musings, for example, with Henry's first lines in Act IV, which could scarcely be blunter or more realistic:

> Gloucester, 'tis true that we are in great danger.
> The greater therefore should our courage be.

By such means does Shakespeare take the "old" story of Agincourt, which the audience knew by heart and which had already been staged three or four times during the preceding decade, and invest it with a new, profound meaning.

Study Questions

1. Where are the French during this scene?
2. What is the subject of discussion among the French?
3. Who says his horse is "pure air and fire"?
4. Do the others agree with him?
5. To what human being does the Constable compare the Dauphin's horse?
6. Why does the punning, joking, and verbal jousting seem odd or inappropriate here?
7. About whose virtue does the Constable say, "never anybody saw it but his lackey"?

8. What metaphor does Rambures use in acknowledging the valor of the English?

9. According to Rambures, what meals are the English served by their wives?

10. What does he mean by this metaphor?

Answers

1. They are camped in the region of Agincourt, a short distance from the English.

2. They debate the relative merits of their horses.

3. The Dauphin makes this extravagant claim.

4. They pretend to agree, but really make fun of him.

5. He likens it to his mistress.

6. They are about to enter battle, yet they waste their time in silly wordplay.

7. This is one of his disparaging references to the Dauphin, whom the Constable despises.

8. He refers to dogs "of umatchable courage."

9. They "give them great meals of beef and iron and steel."

10. He means that they are supported by their wives, which makes them strong and hardy.

Suggested Essay Topics

1. The Dauphin, like the other commanders, was mounted during battle. In light of the crushing defeat the French are about to suffer, what irony do you see in his speeches here? How might his attitude typify that of the French generally? Dramatically speaking, how does it set up the battle itself?

2. What is the value of having one character in this scene disagree with the others about the valor of the English? How do his speeches draw out the others and reveal their attitudes? Without such a character, would the others be as believable?

Act IV

Prologue

Summary

In a subdued, less lyrical style, Chorus asks the audience to imagine the two warring camps during the night before the battle. He describes, on the English side, whispering sentinels, neighing horses, and noisy armor-makers—but on the other side, the "confident and overlusty French" playing dice. He then fortells the action, in which Henry, disguised, passes among the troops and "Bids them good morrow with a modest smile,/And calls them brothers, friends, and countrymen." Finally, the Chorus apologizes for the inadequacy of the stage in enacting this historic tale, saying:

> we shall much disgrace
> With four of five most vile and ragged foils [props, stage swords]
> Right ill-disposed in brawl ridiculous,
> The name of Agincourt.

Analysis

This speech is marked by vivid imagery. Night is personified as a "foul womb." Likewise, "fire answers fire" as the two camps oppose one another, and "Each battle sees the other's umbered face." Night is then likened to a "foul and ugly witch [who] doth limp/So tediously away." Note that the time is three o'clock.

Note, too, that the French are seen gambling, as was also the case in the preceding scene. This will have important philosophical meaning at the climax of the battle.

Study Questions

1. What preparations for war does Chorus describe?

2. Are the two camps far apart?

3. What time is it?

4. Which soldiers are gambling?

5. What are the English soldiers doing?

6. What is implied about the physical condition of the English?

7. What appearance does Henry present to the men? Why?

8. Who is called "Harry"?

9. When will the battle begin?

10. At this point, how do the English chances look?

Answers

1. He describes the noise of armor, the neighing of horses, and the whispers of sentinels.

2. No, they are quite near each other.

3. The time is 3:00 a.m.

4. The French commanders are playing dice.

5. They are sitting and ruminating.

6. The description implies that they are sick, tired, hungry, and ragged.

7. He is cheerful and confident, in order to bolster their morale.

8. This is an informal name for Henry.

9. It will begin on the following day.

10. The weakened English seem sure to lose the battle.

Suggested Essay Topics

1. So far we have seen Henry only as a statesman. How will this act reveal him as a human being? What attitudes and feelings would we expect to see among the soldiers, judging from the physical descriptions here?

2. Discuss the imagery of the sun and the moon in this speech. What does each one refer to? What does it imply about the subject? How are these images used to oppose and highlight each other? Write a comparison-contrast theme discussing these matters.

Act IV, Scene 1

New Characters:

John Bates, Alexander Court, Michael Williams: *soldiers in Henry's army*

Sir Thomas Erpingham: *an officer in Henry's army*

Summary

As predicted in the Prologue, Henry spends most of this scene in disguise, mingling with the common soldiers to sense their morale and spread encouragement.

He borrows a cloak from Sir Thomas Erpingham, an elderly officer, and soon encounters Pistol. Not seeing through the disguise, Pistol treats Henry brusquely. Upon hearing that he is a friend of his adversary Fluellen, he makes a vulgar gesture and exits. Half hidden, Henry then sees Gower and Fluellen himself, who chides his fellow Welshman for making too much noise. The king remarks that Fluellen, though "a little out of fashion," has "much care and valor" in him.

Next, Henry is accosted by three common soldiers, John Bates, Alexander Court, and Michael Williams. When a debate arises as to the nature of the kingship, Henry asserts that "the King is but a man as I am," pointing out that except for "ceremony," all his "senses have but human conditions." The discussion shifts to the philosophical question of whether a king bears responsibility for the moral state of soldiers who die in battle. Bates suggests that he does. "If his cause be wrong, our obedience to the King wipes the crime of it out of us." Henry dissents strongly, insisting that "The King is not bound to answer the particular endings of his soldiers . . . for they purpose not their death when they purpose their service. Every subject's duty is the King's, but every subject's soul is his own." Williams supports this view, saying, "every man that dies ill, the ill upon his own head; the King is not to answer it."

Nevertheless, Henry picks a quarrel with Williams a moment later. Because the time is not right to settle it, the two exchange gloves and agree to meet after the battle. Both put the "gages" in their caps as a sign of recognition.

Once the others depart, Henry soliloquizes on the cost, in personal terms, of kingship. Using the royal "we," to mean himself, he says "We must bear all. O hard condition," and, questioning the value of "ceremony," he concludes that even a "wretched slave . . . with a body filled and vacant mind" sleeps more soundly at night than does a careworn, responsibility-burdened king. But Erpingham's entrance recalls him to the business at hand, and he orders a council of his generals.

The scene concludes with another soliloquy—a prayer to the "god of battles." After pleading for valor on the part of his men, Henry asks God to "think not upon the fault/My father made in compassing the crown." Here he alludes to a crime depicted in Shakespeare's *Richard II*, where his father Henry Bolingbroke unlawfully seized Richard's throne, had himself crowned Henry IV, and caused Richard to be imprisoned and killed.

Analysis

Henry's midnight visit to the troops brings out some of his finest qualities and his modesty, his comradeship with the men, his selfless concern for their feelings. He even tolerates Pistol's ill humor. Shakespeare, having shown Henry's greatness in the roles of king, statesman, judge, and warrior, now shows us his qualities as a man. Henry, though a dutiful adherent to the demands of the throne, never lets the artificialities of office obscure his fundamental humanity.

Despite his virtues, he once again proves somewhat less than perfect. When dealing with Pistol, a man whom he was once friends with for years, he remains in disguise rather than reveal himself. Yet, both might have only hours left to live. What does this secretiveness say about him?

Other questions arise from his dialogue with the three common soldiers. During their lengthy debate and afterward, Henry's reasoning is exceedingly elusive. He begins arguing that a king is just a man, but on the question of responsibility, he holds the king aloof, severing his connection with others. When Williams expresses skepticism about the rightness of the king's cause (unaware, of course, that he is saying this to the king), Henry defensively launches into a lengthy self-justification and then challenges Williams to a fight.

Moreover, in the soliloquy beginning on line 240, Henry laments his own lot, complaining that he has all the burdens of a king, but none of the rewards that even a slave enjoys. (It is also worth noting that the man who now says each man's soul is his own is the same man who, at Harfleur, tacitly approved the raping of women.) Such chameleon-like inconsistency ill befits a "model of the ideal king."

Then, too, there is arguably a strong element of self-pity in him. While a king might legitimately object to the many infringements on his personal liberty, such is not the focus of Henry's soliloquy. He complains instead about not sleeping soundly, enviously contrasting his lot with that of a "wretch," who with a full body and "vacant mind . . . sleeps in Elysium." Responsibilities alone, however, generally cause no loss of sleep—but a guilty conscience does. Might this be what motivates his climactic final soliloquy (line 300)?

As mentioned repeatedly in this guide, Henry's throne is far from secure. Besides the external threats from the rebellious Welsh, Irish, and Scottish, he must also deal with a major problem within England itself, namely, the legitimacy of his throne. Despite the rather torturous claims made by the Archbishop of Canterbury in Act I—and made for the cleric's own self-interest, at that—his father's overthrow of Richard II was, in fact, a naked act of treason. And in this soliloquy, Henry's most deeply personal utterance, we indeed see a guilty conscience—so guilty, in fact, that he has had

Richard's body reburied in pomp and splendor. He has "Five hundred poor . . . in yearly pay/Who twice a day their withered hands hold up/Toward heaven to pardon blood," and he has "built two chantries [chapels] . . . where the sad and solemn priests/Still sing for Richard's soul."

The evidence here strongly suggests that the virtuous, capable, "public" Henry is at least partially a facade behind which lurks a guilt-ridden, insecure man. Consider, too, his denial of friendship with Pistol, which was the third such act (the others relating to Bardolph and Falstaff). This adds to the pattern of threes that pervades the play: the English king has three advisors, as does the French king; there are also three rogues, three common soldiers, and other such groupings; counting an overture in Act IV, Henry is thrice tempted to abandon the war by either surrendering or paying a ransom; and this scene takes place at 3:00 a.m. The present denial of Pistol, besides aligning with the internal pattern, ironically parallels a famous biblical story, Peter's three denials of Jesus on the eve of the crucifixion.

Study Questions

1. Why does Henry adopt a disguise?

2. When Henry asks Pistol for his opinion of the king, is the reply positive or negative?

3. Have Henry and Pistol known each other before?

4. What is Henry's opinion of Fluellen?

5. Do any of the soldiers voice disapproval of King Henry?

6. Henry argues that every subject's duty belongs to the king, but "his ___ is his own." What word is missing?

7. In Henry's dispute with Williams, what sign of recognition do the two exchange?

8. According to Henry, what prevents a king from getting a good night's sleep?

9. For whom has Henry hired 500 people to pray?

10. To whom does Henry admit feelings of guilt for Richard's death?

Answers

1. He wants to pass for a common soldier in order to see how his men are feeling.

2. Positive. He says Henry has a "heart of gold," is a "lad of life," etc.

3. Yes, they were companions during Henry's younger days.

4. He thinks there is "much care and valor" in him.

5. No, they are united in support of him.

6. The word is *soul.*

7. A glove, gauntlet, or gage is the signal.

8. He has too many responsibilities.

9. They pray for Richard II, whom Henry's father unjustly overthrew.

10. To God—he says this during a prayer.

Suggested Essay Topics

1. Noting the pattern of threesomes in the play, see if you can find a few additional examples among characters, images, or events. Discuss these, together with the ones mentioned in the analysis above, in an essay. How are they used as unifying devices? How do they give structure to the overall design and continuity to the action?

2. Henry expresses guilt for the misdeeds of his father, but none for his own failings. Skeptics might argue that this exemplifies the psychological phenomenon of "displacement"—that is, relieving oneself of unacceptable feelings by transposing them onto someone else. Following this line of thought, what sins might Henry actually be feeling guilty about? Consider his relationships with others, his claim to the French throne, and the legal sentences he has imposed or upheld.

Act IV, Scene 2

New Characters:

Lord Grandpre: *a French noble and military commander*

Lord Beaumont: *a French noble and military commander*

Summary

The scene returns to the French camp as the sun rises, signal-ing the beginning of the battle. While the Dauphin and other offic-ers mount up, mention is again made of the the enemy's pitiful condition, and again we see their self-assurance. Constable says they need only take the field and their mere presence will scare the English to death:

> Do but behold yond poor and starved band,
> And your [i.e., the nobles'] fair show shall suck away their souls,
> Leaving them but the shales and husks of men.

To this is added a lengthy speech by another officer, Grandpre, characterizing the foe as men already dead.

Analysis

In this brief, final look at the cocksure French, Grandpre's speech has thematic importance. Religious references and bibli-cal allusions abound in the play, both in the dialogue—there are scores of invocations to God—and in actions such as the preced-ing scene. Here, Grandpre raises a theme that is pervasive in the Bible and central to Christian theology: death and rebirth. The Frenchman calls the English "carrions"—that is corpses—and de-scribes them at length in similarly ghoulish terms. This sets up the climax of the play, in which the "ragged," "beggared" English come back from certain death and are metaphorically reborn in victory.

Study Questions

1. What does Constable say will "suck away the souls" of the English?

2. According to Grandpre, what is the state of the English army?

3. What are "carrions"?

4. What is the mood of these French commanders?

5. What irony is there in their attitude?

6. Do the French commanders fight on foot?

7. According to the Constable, what could the French lackeys and peasants do?

8. How does Grandpre describe the English horses?

9. What mocking suggestion does the Dauphin make?

10. What time of day is it?

Answers

1. He says the mere sight of the French will do so.

2. He describes them as dead men.

3. Carrions are corpses.

4. They are confident of their victory.

5. The audience knows they are about to be defeated.

6. No, they are mounted for battle.

7. He says they could defeat the English all by themselves.

8. He says they are drooping, weak, tired, and generally spent.

9. He suggests that they should feed the starving English first, then fight them.

10. It is dawn.

Suggested Essay Topics

1. Amplify on the death-rebirth theme in an analytic essay. Examine Grandpre's speech closely and apply it to the subsequent action of the play. In doing so, identify an important hero from the New Testament who undergoes the death-rebirth process and compare/contrast him with a major figure from this play.

2. How are horses used as metaphors for the soldiers who ride them? Compare the Dauphin's description of his horse with his personality. Contrast this with Grandpre's description of the English horses. What more do we learn from this imagery?

Act IV, Scene 3

Summary

As if echoing Grandpre's speech, the English officers prepare for death by bidding one another good-bye. Then Henry delivers a speech about the honor of dying for one's country. Suiting his remarks to the occasion, he says the coming battle will become a national holiday celebrating "St. Crispin." (In Catholic theology, October 25 was a feast day for two Roman brothers, Crispinus and Crispianus, who were the patron saints of shoemakers.) And in a famous passage, Henry addresses the men—outnumbered five to one by the French—as

> We few, we happy few, we band of brothers;
> For he today that sheds his blood with me
> Shall be my brother. . . .

As the troops begin to deploy, the French herald Montjoy rides up with a message from King Charles. For the third time he offers an alternative to battle, saying that Henry can spare his army "certain overthrow" by paying a ransom. Once again, the king rejects him, instead making himself the prize:

> Come thou no more for ransom, gentle herald.
> They shall have none, I swear, but these my joints. . . .

Analysis

The St. Crispin's Day speech, which still stirs patriotic passion in the British heart, is the centerpiece of this scene. Some critics have detected a whiff of self-aggrandisement in Henry's assertion that "I am not covetous for gold . . . But if it be a sin to covet honor, / I am the most offending soul alive." But such possible faults fade before the speech as a whole, which brilliantly transforms the army's most grievous problem—its tiny size—into a virtue of the highest order. He speaks confidently, dropping the hesitancy of when he was in disguise. Promising his men this battle will raise them socially to gentlemen and even confer a kind of immortality, making their names "as familiar as household words." He says that "gentlemen in England now abed / Shall think themselves accursed they were not here." As in his speech at the gates of Harfleur, he is the great unifier of his often fractious people, dispensing with class distinctions and welding the army into one, single-minded fighting force. Henry's leadership is masterful, whatever his motives may be.

In confronting Montjoy, too, Henry rises to the heights. His religious references, a constant feature of the dialogue, become even more pronounced, as when he compares the overconfident King Charles to a man in the Bible who sold a lion's skin before killing the lion and was then himself killed during the hunt. And in an elaborate metaphor that echoes the death-rebirth theme, he says that even slain English soldiers, "though buried in your dunghills . . . shall be famed," because their bodies will give off fumes that will rise up through the earth, "breed a plague in France," and kill again "in relapse of mortality."

Study Questions

1. How many is "threescore thousand"?

2. About how many English troops are there in Henry's army?

3. What is Henry "covetous" for?

4. On what saint's day does the Battle of Agincourt occur?

5. Why does Henry say his men are "happy"?

6. What offer does Montjoy make to Henry?

7. Why does Henry liken King Charles to a man in the Bible who sold a lion's skin?

8. How many times has Montjoy negotiated with Henry?

9. Why does Charles have reason to think that Henry will pay a ransom?

10. What counteroffer does Henry repeat to Montjoy?

Answers

1. It is 60,000.

2. About one-fifth of the French army's total, or 12,000.

3. He covets honor.

4. It falls on St. Crispin's Day.

5. They have the chance to win eternal honor in fighting for England.

6. He says Henry can avoid battle by paying a ransom.

7. Both men were overconfident, acting before they had secured their prize.

8. This is the third such time.

9. Henry and his army are outnumbered and are in poor condition.

10. He offers his own body ("joints") as ransom.

Suggested Essay Topics

1. Examine lines 103-113 carefully. How might this passage be considered an answer to Grandpre's speech in the preceding scene, where he likens the English army to a collection of corpses? How might it extend and enlarge the death-rebirth theme implied by that speech? Use specific references to illustrate your argument.

2. Contrast Henry's "St. Crispin's Day" speech with his "imitate the tiger" speech at the gates of Harfleur (III, 1). Which is more elevated and noble? Which is more effective, and why? How do both speeches rhetorically combine religious, nationalistic, and personal appeals into a unified whole?

Act IV, Scene 4

Summary

The battle having begun, a French soldier captured by Pistol pleads for his life. His words are translated by the boy. After much confusion and haggling, Pistol agrees to accept a ransom of 200 gold coins.

Analysis

In light of the ransom at stake in the previous scene, this scene can be considered a companion piece to it. Morally speaking, of course, it is a mirror opposite. Far from rejecting the notion of a ransom, the mercenary-minded Pistol is more than eager to accept. (Buying one's release was so common during Shakespeare's time that it was frequently the chief source of an army's income.) His inverted sense of values is also reflected in the dialogue where he mistakes a reference to God ("O Seigneur Dieu!") for the victim's name.

As in another companion piece, the scene at the Harfleur wall, Pistol converts a serious theme into parody. Here it is the concept of mercy—a virtue repeatedly associated with Henry. Pistol equates the virtue with his own parasitic nature. "As I suck blood, I will some mercy show." Not surprisingly, the remark elicits disgust from the boy, who says, "I did never know so full a voice issue from so empty a heart."

Study Questions

1. What is the French soldier afraid of?

2. How does he hope to save himself?

3. What is Pistol's reaction?

4. Who translates for the Frenchman?

5. What is the boy's reaction to these proceedings?

6. When the Frenchman cries "O Seigneur Dieu!," what is his meaning?

7. How does Pistol mistake his meaning?

8. How does the action of this scene parallel that of the pre-
    ceding scene?

9. Why do you think Shakespeare has the boy translate in this
    scene?

10. What "luggage" does the boy decide to help guard?

Answers

1. He is afraid Pistol will kill him.

2. He hopes to bribe Pistol to let him go.

3. He refuses at first, then agrees.

4. The boy translates.

5. He is disgusted by them.

6. He is invoking God ("Oh Lord God!").

7. He thinks the man is stating his name.

8. Both involve a ransom.

9. So he will realize Pistol's lies and double-dealing.

10. This refers to the possessions of the soldiers now in the field.

Suggested Essay Topics

1. Note the boy's decision to "stay with the lackeys" and guard
    the soldiers' luggage. What does this, coming from a former
    henchman of thieves, tell us about the change in his char-
    acter?

2. Pistol suggests an equation between "sucking blood" and
    showing mercy. Because mercy is the virtue most strongly
    associated with Henry, the implication is that in some ways
    Pistol is a moral opposite of him. See if you can think of two
    or three other instances in which the two reflect each other's
    character. Discuss them in a comparison-contrast essay.

Act IV, Scene 5

Summary

In the play's shortest scene, the French nobles are found routed and panic-stricken. Their army's ranks broken and facing certain defeat, they decide to seek death in battle rather than the disgrace they have earned. Bourbon speaks for all in vowing to throw himself on the enemy's spear when he says, "I'll to the throng./Let life be short, else shame will be too long."

Analysis

Despite its brevity, this climactic scene has one moment of special significance. It is the Dauphin's invocation of Fortune, a mythological goddess who was thought to control the lives of humans. In contrast to the prayers of Henry and his men, which are consistently directed to God, this blasphemous act associates the Frenchman with a pagan deity. Once again, Shakespeare underscores the different value systems of the two peoples, with the spiritual, high-minded English on one side, and the luxury-loving French on the other.

Perhaps to underscore the point, the Dauphin asks "Be these the wretches that we played dice for?" (In the previous scene, he and the others had placed wagers on the number of English soldiers they would kill.) In the Elizabethan world view, to forsake Christianity and follow Fortune was the sure way to damnation, and Shakespeare's audience would not have missed the implications of his words—nor would they have overlooked the Constable's reference to "Disorder."

Study Questions

1. What three authorities are invoked at the start of this scene?

2. What does the French "ranks are broke" mean?

3. What do these Frenchmen intend to do?

4. What motivates them to do so?

5. If they decide to live, what is their probable future?

6. How does their state of mind here compare with the way we last saw them?

7. What suggestion does the Dauphin make?

8. Do the English now outnumber the French?

9. How does this fact make their behavior all the more shameful?

10. Why is the Dauphin's reaction more shameful than that of the others?

Answers

1. The French call on the Devil, the Lord, and the goddess Fortune.

2. It means discipline has broken down and the army is in flight.

3. They go to commit suicide by reentering the battle.

4. They are ashamed of this humiliating defeat.

5. They face disgrace, as shown earlier in the play after the Harfleur loss.

6. Their state of mind is the exact opposite of the smug overconfidence we last saw.

7. He proposes suicide by saying, "Let's stab ourselves."

8. No. Orleans says, "We are enough yet living in the field/To smother up the English."

9. Even with a vast numerical superiority they are losing.

10. They will at least go down fighting the enemy, not by their own hand.

Suggested Essay Topics

1. Look up the entry for "shame" in the dictionary. How are its various meanings applicable to the French? Write an essay defining the word in terms of the play.

2. Look up "dishonor" and do the same. In what ways are the meanings of this word *not* applicable? Write an essay discussing this important difference.

Act IV, Scene 6

Summary

Elsewhere in the field, Henry, in the thick of the fight, receives word that the dukes of York and Suffolk have both been killed. Exeter recounts their final moments, in which the two soldiers embraced in "a testament of noble-ending love." But Henry has no time for grieving. Notified that the enemy has rallied, he issues the order that "every soldier kill his prisoners."

Analysis

Henry's command to murder all French captives has stirred perhaps more controversy than any other single line of the play. To some, this is a barbarous, indefensible act of cruelty, contradicting all the magnanimity implied by his fine speeches. Certainly it is a radical move and, in the context of Exeter's lofty sentiments, a jarring reversal in tone.

As will shortly be explained, the line's placement is perhaps the result of an unfortunate textual error. But what if it is not? What conclusions can we draw from the text as it stands? Henry's only discernible motivation—the news that "The French have reinforced their scattered men"—is hardly a justification for slaughtering unarmed captives. Should this scene have been as Shakespeare intended, it offers the play's most damning evidence against Henry, portraying him as the worst kind of coward with, quite literally, a take-no-prisoners attitude. The condemnation is compounded by the preceding half of the scene, in which Exeter relates the deaths of York and Suffolk. It is difficult to imagine a greater emotional contrast than that between the poignant end of two noble warriors and the truculent command of a panicky, vindictive leader.

Study Questions

1. What values do the deaths of York and Suffolk exemplify?
2. How might their death be contrasted with the French in the preceding scene?
3. Why would killing prisoners be considered barbaric and dishonorable?

4. Why does Henry give this order?

5. What effect might this have on the audience's estimation of Henry?

6. Does Henry know the battle's outcome yet?

7. How many times did Exeter see York during the battle?

8. When Suffolk saw York die, what did he do?

9. What is Exeter's emotional response to this memory?

10. Does this news suggest that the English are winning or losing?

Answers

1. They show courage, valor, and the soldier's honorable love for his comrade in arms.

2. The French are seen to be cowards, killing themselves rather than suffering disgrace.

3. The prisoners are defenseless.

4. He hears that the French have rallied.

5. It might lower him in their esteem.

6. No, he does not.

7. Exeter saw him fall and rise again three times.

8. He embraced and kissed him and said a farewell.

9. Exeter weeps.

10. This suggests that they are losing.

Suggested Essay Topics

1. Consider the scene described by Exeter—military valor at the moment of death—in the context of the French commanders' behavior. What values do the final moments of York and Suffolk seem to exemplify? How do they compare or contrast with those of the French?

2. Exeter says he saw York fall and rise three times: "Thrice within this hour/I saw him down, thrice up again and fighting." Note, too, Henry's reference to "thrice-valiant country-

men." Discuss a possible parallel between York's valor and that of Henry, who is thrice tempted to give up his plans to conquer France.

3. What might Shakespeare's audience have thought of Henry's vengeful order? Might they have supported it as a necessary consequence of warfare, or might they have despised him? How might the emotional climate of the play have been affected?

Act IV, Scene 7

Summary

Fluellen and Gower, upon hearing of Henry's command, are both highly pleased. Fluellen compares the king to Alexander the Great, paralleling Alexander's murder of a friend with Henry's rejection of Falstaff.

At this point the king himself arrives and repeats his order to "cut the throats of those we have." He adds, "not one of them that we shall take / Shall taste our mercy."

Just then Montjoy returns, bearing a request that the French be allowed to bury their dead. Henry asks if the outcome of the battle has been decided, and the herald answers, "The day is yours." "Praised be God, and not our strength, for it!" cries the happy king.

Henry and Fluellen then spend a few moments discussing the fact that they are fellow countrymen, Henry being from the Welsh town of Monmouth. In the remainder of the scene, the subplot involving Henry and Williams is resumed. When the king notices his glove in the soldier's cap, he engineers a prank by sending Williams away and then giving Fluellen the other man's glove (after first claiming that he, Henry, had stolen it from a soldier named Alencon). Fluellen, with the gage in his cap, is then sent on the same errand as was Williams, unwittingly to antagonize him. Once he is gone, however, Henry admits that "I by bargain should / Wear it myself," and he sends his brother Gloucester and Warwick after Fluellen to prevent further "mischief."

Analysis

This scene contains some clues that could account for Henry's apparently rash, unjustified order to kill the prisoners. The first is Fluellen's revelation, in the opening lines, that the French have slain all the English boys guarding the camp's luggage. This intelligence comes directly after the kill-all-prisoners order. Had it come just before, Henry's motivation would be clear. Besides being "expressly against the law of arms," as Fluellen says, the killing of the boys is an egregious atrocity, and probably reason enough for Henry to retaliate in kind.

Note, too, that Henry's next appearance begins with the apparently unmotivated line, "I was not angry since I came to France/ Until this instant," whereupon he reissues the murderous command. Were the script rearranged, however, and this speech coupled with Fluellen's revelation, it would become perfectly understandable. (History bears this out: the slaughter of the boys did in fact precede—and prompt—the killing of the prisoners.)

Misplaced lines? Quite possibly. Despite centuries of scholarly reconstruction, textual mistakes are by no means uncommon in Shakespeare's plays. At a time long before copyright protection, scripts were amended freely by actors, directors, managers, printers, and various other interested parties, so it is altogether possible that a mix-up occurred here. Accordingly, many contemporary directors take out the Williams subplot altogether.

Returning to our thematic discussion, the boy occupies a special position in the play vis-à-vis Henry. Remember that Henry's youth is one of the defining features of his character. Part of his task in being king is proving that he has cast off his wayward habits and reached a sober maturity. Yet he *is* still young, and to that extent has a certain affinity with this boy—who, after all, has followed in his footsteps by falling in with Falstaff and his crew. Just as the Dauphin is the alter ego of Henry the man, the boy is the alter ego of Henry the child.

Throughout the play, however, the two have been moving along opposite paths. Henry, in making difficult and often morally ambiguous decisions, has been gradually losing his innocence, while the boy, by renouncing Pistol and the others, has effectively reclaimed his. The change from henchman to guardian tells us as

much, and so, perhaps, does his generic, even allegorical name. Psychologically, what could be more shattering to Henry than the death of his "other self"? And what could more impel him to completely abandon mercy, the trait that links him most closely with his now-lost innocence?

The remainder of the scene, which deals with Henry's prank on Williams, is likewise controversial. Those who consider it an important passage point out that Williams was grossly insubordinate in saying earlier, that the king "may be ransomed and we ne'er the wiser"—that is, that Henry might be deceiving his soldiers. During wartime, in fact, such a remark might even be treasonous. According to this view, Henry, in setting up a feud between Williams and Fluellen, is reminding Williams that he might have paid for the comment with his life. As a consequence, the incident repeats the clash, seen at least twice before, between mercy (in the form of a pardon) and justice.

Others disagree, arguing that the prank is not only rather tedious and unfunny, but also wholly unbecoming of a king, particularly one as mindful of the dignity and majesty of his office as Henry. They also argue that, from a dramatic standpoint, it could hardly be more inappropriate. Coming just after an historic military victory—at the very climax—the prank plunges the play into bathos and totally dissipates its emotional energy. Finally, they point out that the story is continued in the succeeding scene, which suggests that the break might originally have come earlier, at about line 124, where Henry dispatches some heralds to count the casualties. Such a break would create a more natural division between the high seriousness of warfare and the low comedy that tends to undercut it.

Study Questions

1. What explanation could be offered to explain or justify Henry's order to kill the prisoners?

2. What change would be wrought by a rearrangement of the script?

3. What key piece of information is given at the start of this scene?

4. What special significance might this have for Henry?

5. What clue do we get that the event has affected him deeply?

6. To what does Henry attribute his victory?

7. What action occurs after the victory?

8. Why does Henry have Fluellen wear one of Williams' gloves in his cap?

9. Where does Henry say he got the glove?

10. What does he expect to happen when the two men meet?

Answers

1. It probably stems from a textual error, or a mix-up in the sequence of events.

2. Seen in proper sequence, the events would motivate Henry's order.

3. Fluellen says the French have murdered the boys guarding the luggage.

4. His friend, the boy, was among those slain.

5. He says, "I was not angry . . . until this instant" and repeats the order.

6. Henry says it was the hand of God.

7. A subplot is resumed, in which Henry plays a prank on Williams.

8. He wants Williams to mistake him for the disguised Henry of Act III.

9. Henry says he stole it from another soldier.

10. He expects that there will be a fight.

Suggested Essay Topics

1. In outline form, rearrange the events of this episode according to the order suggested in the *Analysis* above. Include key lines of dialogue showing the characters' states of mind. Then briefly discuss how this affects the emotional pitch of the scene. How does the new arrangement heighten the tension just before the climax?

2. Using the same technique as in question one, write an outline omitting the Henry-Fluellen-Williams subplot. Skip forward from Act IV, Scene 7, line 95 to Act IV, Scene 8, line 76. What effects does this have on the overall mood? How does it intensify the climax and sustain the denouement? What is lost by the omission? What other omissions would be needed to eliminate this subplot entirely?

3. Write an argumentation essay supporting a serious interpretation of the Henry-Fluellen-Williams subplot. What legal issues are at stake in the quarrel between the king and Williams? What moral issues? Depending on the outcome of the quarrel, how is our judgment of Henry likely to be affected?

Act IV, Scene 8

Summary

The final scene concludes the action between Henry and Williams. Mistaking Fluellen for the disguised Henry he met earlier, the soldier strikes the officer, an act for which he is immediately accused of treason. Warwick and Gloucester arrive too late to prevent the blow, but after a moment Henry enters and explains everything. By way of pardoning Williams, he fills his glove with crowns.

An English herald enters with an account of the casualties. Some 10,000 Frenchmen died during the battle, but only about 25 Englishmen died. In light of this seemingly miraculous discrepancy, Henry once more attributes the victory to divine intervention, and he prescribes the death penalty for any soldier who boasts of it or "take[s] that praise from God/Which is His only." The scene, and the act, ends with the singing of hymns.

Analysis

The Williams subplot is resolved in this episode. The soldier's crime, says Henry, stems from his earlier threat to strike him—a treasonous act for which Fluellen now says, "let his neck answer for it." This recapitulates the offense mentioned early in the play where a drunken man made an insulting remark (see Act II, Scene

1). In pardoning Williams, Henry rounds out the action and reestablishes the rule of mercy. A parallel may also be seen with the two other cases in which he was called upon to pass judgment, over the three spies at Southampton and over the thief Bardolph. If anyone found him too unforgiving then, he clearly redeems himself. This final act of clemency seals our impression of him as a man of greatness both spiritually and militarily.

As for the presumed "miracle" of the Agincourt victory, history offers a less exalted (but equally intriguing) explanation. The English fought from fortified positions, behind palisades which the French knights' horses could not penetrate, so few fell beneath the cavalry's spears. On the other hand, the English archers were heavily supplied with armor-piercing arrows, which they could shoot accurately from a distance of hundreds of feet. In the open fields of Agincourt, the slow-moving chevaliers were virtually defenseless against them. A massacre was all but inevitable.

Exercising dramatic license, however, Shakespeare allows the theological interpretation to dominate. Nothing in the last moments of the scene are particularly unusual except, perhaps, the vehemence of Henry's piety. Even in Elizabethan England, death seems a disproportionate penalty simply for boasting. As always, a trace of disingenuousness lingers. Is the good, wise, ever-so-considerate king perhaps overplaying his part?

Study Questions

1. What happens when Fluellen meets Williams?
2. How does this dispute end?
3. In round numbers, what are the casualties of the battle on both sides?
4. What are *Non Nobis* and *Te Deum*?
5. Why does Henry order his men to sing them?
6. Why does Fluellen take Williams for a traitor?
7. Is Williams reconciled with Fluellen by the gift of money?
8. Does Henry apologize for having deceived Williams and Fluellen?

9. Did many of the French ruling class die in the battle?

10. What penalty does Henry prescribe for boasting of victory?

Answers

1. Williams strikes him.

2. Henry admits his prank and gives Williams gold coins.

3. There are some 10,000 French dead and about 25 English dead.

4. They are hymns praising God.

5. He is convinced the victory was a miracle.

6. Under military law, when a soldier strikes an officer, he is usually guilty of treason.

7. Probably not, since he rejects the offer.

8. No, he does not.

9. Yes, some 9,000 were princes, nobles, and knights.

10. Henry makes it punishable by death.

Suggested Essay Topics

1. Henry's subdued behavior after the victory is far different from the wild exultation one might expect from a triumphant army commander. Though understandable in terms of his pious deference to God, it may have other causes instead. What less noble, more pragmatic reasons might he have for downplaying this moment? Consider three aspects of the play: (1) the possibility that his claim on the French throne was never valid to begin with; (2) his impending marriage to the French princess; and (3) his desire to escape his earlier reputation as a rowdy, party-loving wastrel.

2. Here, as elsewhere, the subplot involving Williams' earlier meeting with Henry seems to contradict other elements of the play. Support this proposition in an essay, focusing on the following observations: (1) the action interrupts the logical flow of events from Henry's learning of their victory to

the report of battle casualties; (2) staging a practical joke like this is unseemly for a king, especially one as conscious of his public image as is Henry; and (3) in contrast to his magnanimity toward the French people, here he never bothers to apologize to either Fluellen or Williams for deceiving them. Moreover, his "payoff" in gold coins seems a crass substitute for genuine repentance.

Act V

Prologue

Summary

Apologizing yet again for "th' excuse/Of time, of numbers, and due course of things,/Which cannot in their huge and proper life/Be here represented," Chorus relates the events that have transpired between the fall of France and the action of Act 5. Henry returned to England and a tumultuous reception, the Holy Roman Emperor also made the journey in an unsuccessful attempt to impose a peace treaty on England and France. Henry came back to Paris to claim the spoils of war, the French throne, and Princess Katharine.

Analysis

As elsewhere in the play, similes by Chorus compare Henry and the English to the heroes of classical times. Here, the welcoming Mayor of London "and all his brethren" are "like to the senators of th' antique Rome/With the plebeians swarming at their heels," while the king is "their conqu'ring Caesar."

Chorus also adds a contemporary note in referring to a "general" under "our gracious empress" (i.e., Queen Elizabeth I) who returned from Ireland "bringing rebellion broached on his sword." This general would be one of two heroes of Shakespeare's time, either Exeter or Mountjoy, who crushed an Irish uprising in 1599. The reference would serve as a salute both to the Queen, who was the playwright's chief patron, and to the patriotic pride of the audience.

Study Questions

1. What geographic locales are mentioned in the Prologue?

2. What is a whiffler?

3. What does the metaphor of a whiffler refer to here?

4. What do Henry's "bruised helmet and bent sword" signify?

5. What do his advisors want Henry to do with these objects?

6. What is his answer to them? Why?

7. Why does Henry delay in taking over the French throne?

8. To whom or what are the London mayor and citizens compared?

9. What does Henry's rejection of glory tell us about him?

10. Why did Shakespeare not stage the homecoming scene?

Answers

1. Calais, the English beach, London (Blackheath), and France are mentioned.

2. This is a person who prepares the way for a king or queen.

3. It refers to the crowds on the English beach, welcoming Henry home.

4. They signify his bravery and ruggedness in battle.

5. They want Henry to present them to the people as tokens of victory.

6. He refuses, saying the credit should go to God.

7. France is undergoing a period of national mourning for their army's defeat.

8. They are compared to the senators and plebians of classical Rome.

9. It shows his humility and piety in giving God credit for the victory.

10. The stage could probably not do justice to such a large, overwhelming event.

Suggested Essay Topics

1. How might a film director overcome some of the limitations faced by Shakespeare in handling the return of Henry to England? Copy the Prologue, inserting scenes, vignettes, or camera shots that would dramatize the events described.

2. In plays and movies, the intent is often to suggest a parallel between historical events and those of the present day. What effect would Shakespeare likely have intended by his contemporary references here to Queen Elizabeth ("our gracious empress") and an English general recently returning from suppressing an Irish rebellion? Could the Battle of Agincourt (1415) be compared to the defeat of the Spanish armada (1588)? Are other parallels possible?

Act V, Scene 1

Summary

Back in France, in the English camp, Fluellen is seen wearing a leek in his cap. Questioned by Gower, he says he means to force-feed this pungent object to "the rascally, scald, beggarly, lousy, pragging knave Pistol," who had earlier insulted his heritage by making wisecracks about the leek, which happens to be the Welsh national emblem.

When Pistol enters, Fluellen makes good his intention by thrashing him soundly with a cudgel, or short, heavy club. Though he eats the leek, Pistol is unrepentant, and once the other has left he mutters, "All hell shall stir for this."

When Gower, too, exits, the rogue reflects on his current status. Word has reached him that his wife Hostess Quickly has died of "a malady of France—that is, syphilis. Now alone, beaten, and penniless, he resolves to go home and resume a life of crime when he says "to England I'll steal, and there I'll steal."

Analysis

The business about the leek allows Shakespeare to bring the two major comic characters, Pistol and Fluellen, back for a final bow, and

also to establish a light-hearted tone for the last act. Fluellen has perhaps his funniest moments in juxtaposing elaborate politeness with scathing insults. "Aunchient Pistol, you scurvy, lousy knave, God pless you." The scene also continues the theme of unification, as Gower tells Pistol, "You thought because he could not speak English in the native garb, he could not therefore handle an English cudgel. . . . [L]et a Welsh correction teach you a good English condition." Pistol remains in character, however, blaming Fortune for his problems.

Study Questions

1. What events transpired between Acts IV and V?

2. Where has Fluellen placed the leek he intends to force Pistol to eat?

3. How does this parallel the quarrel between Henry and Williams?

4. Besides the beating, what other misfortunes has Pistol suffered?

5. Does he decide to change occupations as a result?

6. Who is described as "swelling like a turkey-cock"?

7. What is Pistol's reaction to the leek?

8. What is a cudgel?

9. During Elizabethan times, was it a compliment to call someone a Trojan?

10. Before leaving, Fluellen gives Pistol a groat. What is this?

Answers

1. Henry came back to England, the Holy Roman Emperor tried unsuccessfully to impose a peace treaty on England and France. Henry returned to Paris to claim his prizes.

2. He wears it in his cap.

3. Each of them wore the other's glove in his cap.

4. Pistol's wife has died and he is poor.

5. No, Pistol remains a thief and a rogue.

6. Pistol is.

7. He says it makes him sick.

8. It is a short, heavy club.

9. No, it was an insult. A Trojan was a dissolute man.

10. It is a cheap coin, comparable to a penny.

Suggested Essay Topics

1. Write a character study of Pistol. Besides establishing his negative qualities, mention scenes here and elsewhere in which Shakespeare makes him at least somewhat sympathetic. Contrast him in this respect with Bardolph and Nym, and contrast his moral character with that of the boy.

2. Fluellen is frequently seen in the play as a somewhat clownish figure, misspeaking himself and behaving foolishly. How does he achieve greater stature here in his closing appearance than he enjoyed earlier? Why is it fitting that he should be the scourge of Pistol, rather than some other character? How is he appropriate for this task?

Act V, Scene 2

Summary

In the French palace, the leaders of England and France meet to settle the terms of a peace treaty. After friendly greetings are exchanged, Burgundy gives a long speech summarizing the political situation. Henry then sends the others off to negotiate these matters while he courts Katharine, with whom he has fallen in love.

His amorous attentions make up most of this final scene. Appealing to her not as a king but as a "plain soldier," he asks for her consent to join their lives and their kingdoms in marriage. Though shy and hesitant at first, she ultimately agrees. When the others return, the French king accedes to this and to "every article" of Henry's other terms. Everyone present greets the reconciliation with joy, and the play ends.

Before the final curtain, Chorus gives a brief epilogue relating the subsequent history of this event. After ruling for but a "small time," Henry died young, leaving the throne to his infant son Henry VI. This king, unwise and unlucky, eventually "lost France and made his England bleed." The play ends with a plea for the audience's acceptance.

Analysis

Though Henry's wooing of Katharine dominates this scene, and properly so, thematically Burgundy's speech is at least as important. Its literal meaning is straightforward enough. He wants to reconcile the leaders of the warring countries and establish a lasting peace. But harking back to a metaphor used earlier, his words have a far deeper significance.

In Shakespeare's time, the state of nature was a state of order. The creator set each earthly thing in its proper place, and it was mankind's responsibility to maintain that arrangement. As long as humans remained virtuous, a general sense of orderliness would prevail, whether in the religious sphere or the secular, whether personal or political, whether individual or collective. To upset the divine plan was to invite disorder—an act of evil.

In Burgundy's speech, the symbol of order is the garden, specifically "this best garden of the world,/Our fertile France." Peace, he says, "hath from France too long been chased," and as a result "all her husbandry [agriculture] doth lie on heaps,/Corrupting in its own fertility." From here he goes on to recount the ills that have befallen his country, in both its vegetation and its people. Restoring the peace would, he implies, heal a breach in nature itself. Thus are the political issues linked to universal principles, and the signing of the treaty takes on an almost cosmic dimension.

Once these affairs of state are disposed of—the king's approval is a forgone conclusion—the focus can shift to the personal level, where Henry wins his lady's love.

Those skeptical of Henry's motives may point out that the marriage, too, is a virtual *fait accompli*, because it is one of the terms of the treaty. This being so, he may be amusing himself at her expense. (Remember, Katharine is only 14 and, from what we have seen, far less sophisticated than this worldly young man.) Yet it is difficult to resist the charm and inventiveness of his lengthy flirtation. When, for example, he claims, "I have no cunning in protestation, only downright oaths," but then launches into a clever, witty series of parallelisms, the obviousness of the deception is humorous rather than damning. So, too, are his pose as a "plain soldier," his fumbling attempts at French, and his unconvincing self-deprecations.

Indeed, his ability to indulge in such playfulness marks an important change, because it is perhaps his first sign of total self-confidence. Until now he has fulfilled the roles assigned by his station, and done so with distinction. But here, inspired by a woman of equal charm and spontaneity, he can let down his defenses and begin to establish genuine emotional intimacy. This is a growth process. He graduates from the forms of office to the realities of ordinary life, achieving a maturity as admirable in its way as his accomplishments as soldier and king.

Katharine, too, gains in stature with an impressive display of womanly self-possession. Though clearly beguiled by her suitor, she is not won easily. Nor is she distracted from the consequences of her acts, asking "Is it possible dat I sould love de enemy of France?" Far more than her frivolous brother the Dauphin, she shows an intelligent understanding of the English, and she convincingly emerges as a strong, capable, desirable match for Henry.

In short, Shakespeare, though at times admitting shortcomings in his hero, does not allow them to spoil the festive mood of the last act. As stated in another one of his plays, "Jack shall have Jill, naught shall go ill."

Study Questions

1. What attitude do the attendees of this meeting seem to have?

2. What is the purpose of the conference?

3. The Queen of France likens Henry's eyes to "balls of the burning basilisk." What is a basilisk?

4. What does Burgundy call "this best garden of the world"?

5. What are *docks, kecksies,* and *burrs*?

6. What might they symbolize in Burgundy's "garden"?

7. To overcome Katharine's shyness, how does Henry describe himself?

8. Henry says he has something "not worth sunburning." What is it?

9. Does Charles disagree with any of Henry's treaty demands?

10. How many of Henry's descendants held the French throne after him?

Answers

1. All express goodwill and a positive attitude.

2. The attendees have gathered to sign a peace treaty.

3. It is a type of cannon.

4. He is referring to France.

5. They are varieties of weeds.

6. They might symbolize disorder, warfare, or evil.

7. He says he is a "plain soldier," not a mighty king.

8. It is his face.

9. No, he consents to everything.

10. Only his son, and he only for a little while.

Suggested Essay Topics

1. Examine Burgundy's speech, and specifically his garden imagery, carefully. Write an essay comparing or contrasting it with one or more other speeches using the same metaphor. Also, tell how Burgundy effectively rounds out this theme and adds a conclusive note to the proceedings. What, finally, does it imply about the future of France under Henry?

2. What aspects of Henry's speeches to Katharine reflect the fact that she is someone scarcely out of childhood? How might his humor, his images, and his overall approach have been different if she were a mature woman? Cite specific lines in support of your conclusions.

SECTION SEVEN

Sample Analytical Paper Topics

The following paper topics are designed to test your understanding of the play as a whole and to analyze important themes and literary devices. Following each question is a sample outline to help get you started.

Topic #1

Henry V is in most respects a model of the ideal king—wise, just, courageous, and kind. Yet there are a number of moments when less praiseworthy qualities seem apparent. It would be an overstatement to say he is a villain, but neither is he as perfect as his surface behavior would indicate. Write an essay showing how the positive qualities in him are to an extent counterbalanced by negative tendencies.

Outline

I.   Thesis Statement: *Although Henry V exhibits the virtues of an ideal English king throughout the play, certain details suggest that some aspects of his nature are less than admirable—indeed, that there are elements of the villain, as well as the hero, in him.*

II. Examples of positive and negative behavior

   A.   Treatment of his friends

      Positive: He shows mercy toward a drunken soldier who insulted him.

Negative: He broke Falstaff's heart by disavowing their earlier friendship.

B. Unmasking of the conspirators Scroop, Grey, and Cambridge

Positive: He cleverly manipulates them into passing judgment on themselves.

Negative: He deviously entraps them rather than forthrightly charging them with treason.

C. Heroism in battle

Positive: He courageously leads the charge into Harfleur and at Agincourt.

Negative: He threatens monstrous punishments at Harfleur—babies spitted on pikes, etc.—and cruelly orders all French captives killed at Agincourt.

D. Compassion

Positive: He weeps at the deaths of York and Suffolk.

Negative: He callously has Bardolph, a former friend, hanged for a minor theft.

E. Personal honesty

Positive: In wooing Katharine, he speaks from his heart as a "plain soldier."

Negative: He knows she is his by right. The soldier act is false and manipulative.

III. Conclusion: Given the inconsistencies in Henry's behavior, it is impossible to regard him simply as an ideal king.

Topic #2

In the language of the theater, a "foil" is a character who serves as a contrast to another, illuminating that character's qualities by exemplifying their opposites. How might the Dauphin be considered a foil to Henry V? Consider three aspects in which this may be true, and tell how Shakespeare establishes this relationship between two figures who actually never meet face to face during the play.

Outline

I.   Thesis Statement: *In* Henry V, *Shakespeare uses the Dauphin as a foil to Henry. First he establishes their similarities, so the audience will compare the two, and then he shows their differences. In doing so, each character highlights the opposite qualities of the other in terms of manners, personality, and leadership.*

II. Similarities

   A. Dauphin is the French prince and heir to the throne; Henry is the English king.

   B. Both are young men.

   C. Both are military commanders.

III. Differences: Manners and Lifestyle

   A. Dauphin speaks in flowery, high-flown speeches; Henry is bluntly realistic.

   B. Dauphin is pampered and coddled; Henry is rough and rugged.

   C. Dauphin communicates by insinuation and insult; Henry communicates by overt, frank opposition.

IV. Differences: Personality

   A. Dauphin is complacent and self-satisfied; Henry risks all for honor.

   B. On the eve of battle, Dauphin thinks only of his pleasures; Henry thinks only of his troops.

   C. Dauphin elicits scorn from his colleagues; Henry elicits respect and admiration.

V.   Differences: Leadership

   A. Dauphin forsakes Harfleur; Henry fights side-by-side with his fellow countrymen.

   B. Dauphin remains aloof from his army; Henry mingles with the men in disguise.

   C. In adversity, Dauphin commits suicide; Henry shows fortitude.

VI.   Conclusion: By their similarities of situation and opposition in manners, personality, and leadership, the Dauphin and Henry complement each other in showing us the whole range of human qualities.

Topic #3

A number of times in *Henry V*, Shakespeare presents similar-looking scenes side-by-side. Because of this juxtaposition, such scenes imply a commentary on the play's characters or issues. Identify three such pairings and explain their significance.

Outline

I.   Thesis Statement: *In* Henry V, *Shakespeare juxtaposes certain scenes so as to create pairs, or companion scenes, that by their relationship comment on the characters and themes. Three telling examples are Act 1, Scene 2 and Act 2, Scene 4; Act 3, Scenes 1 and 2; and Act 4, Scenes 3 and 4.*

II.   First example: Act 1, Scene 2, and Act 2, Scene 4

   A.   In Act 1, Scene 2, King Henry receives counsel from his trusted advisors, and then a messenger enters with a challenge from his enemy the Dauphin.

   B.   In Act 2, Scene 4, King Charles receives counsel from his trusted advisors, and then a messenger enters with a challenge from his enemy Henry.

      1.   Purpose: To contrast the personalities of the two kings and show the unity or disunity of the two royal councils.

III. Second example: Act 3, Scenes 1 and 2

   A.   In Act 3, Scene 1, Henry rallies his troops for a charge at Harfleur, giving a speech beginning "Once more unto the breach, dear friends, once more."

   B.   In Act 3, Scene 2, Pistol gives a similar rallying cry to his comrades: "On, on, on, on, on! To the breach, to the breach!" But he is actually leading a retreat.

      1.   Purpose: To highlight the cowardice and ignominy of Pistol and his companions.

IV. Third example: Act 4, Scenes 3 and 4

    A. At the end of Act 4, Scene 3, the French herald Montjoy demands a ransom from Henry in exchange for sparing the English army annihilation.

    B. In Act 4, Scene 4, Pistol demands a ransom from a captive French soldier in exchange for sparing the man's life.

        1. Purpose: To contrast Henry's noble qualities with Pistol's baseness.

V. Conclusion: By playing one scene off another, Shakespeare uses the dramatic structure to enhance the characterizations in *Henry V* and illuminate some of the main themes.

SECTION EIGHT

Bibliography

Primary Source

Shakespeare, William. *Henry V*, ed. Barbara A. Mowat. *The Folger Shakespeare Library*. New York: Pocket Books, 1995.

Secondary Sources

Boyce, Charles. *Shakespeare A to Z*. New York: Roundtable Press, Inc., 1990.

Halliday, F. E. *A Shakespeare Companion*. New York: Shocken Books, 1964.

Ludowyk, E. F. C. *Understanding Shakespeare*. Cambridge: Cambridge University Press, 1962.

Watt, Homer A., Karl J. Holzknecht, Raymond Ross, *Outlines of Shakespeare's Plays*. New York: Harper Collins, 1970.

Available at your local bookstore or order directly from us by sending in coupon below.

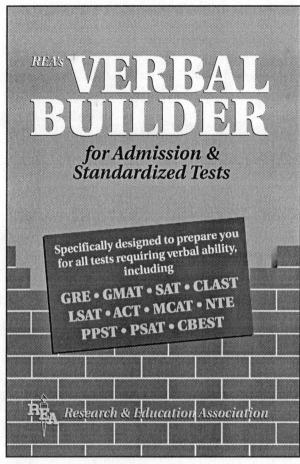

REA's VERBAL BUILDER

for Admission & Standardized Tests

Specifically designed to prepare you for all tests requiring verbal ability, including

GRE • GMAT • SAT • CLAST
LSAT • ACT • MCAT • NTE
PPST • PSAT • CBEST

Research & Education Association

Available at your local bookstore or order directly from us by sending in coupon below.

THE BEST TEST PREPARATION FOR THE

GRE
GRADUATE
RECORD
EXAMINATION

LITERATURE IN ENGLISH

by Pauline Beard, Ph.D. • Thomas C. Kennedy, Ph.D. • Robert Liftig, Ed.D. • James S. Malek, Ph.D.

6 Full-Length Exams

Completely Up-to-Date based on the current format of the GRE Literature in English Test

➤ The ONLY test preparation book with detailed explanations to every exam question

➤ Far more comprehensive than any other test preparation book

Specially designed to depict the most recent GRE exams accurately, in both the type of questions and the level of difficulty

REA *Research & Education Association*

Available at your local bookstore or order directly from us by sending in coupon below

MAXnotes

REA's Literature Study Guides

MAXnotes® are student-friendly. They offer a fresh look at masterpieces of literature, presented in a lively and interesting fashion. **MAXnotes®** offer the essentials of what you should know about the work, including outlines, explanations and discussions of the plot, character lists, analyses, and historical context. **MAXnotes®** are designed to help you think independently about literary works by raising various issues and thought-provoking ideas and questions. Written by literary experts who currently teach the subject, **MAXnotes®** enhance your understanding and enjoyment of the work.

Available **MAXnotes®** include the following:

Absalom, Absalom!	Heart of Darkness	Of Mice and Men
The Aeneid of Virgil	Henry IV, Part I	On the Road
Animal Farm	Henry V	Othello
Antony and Cleopatra	The House on Mango Street	Paradise Lost
As I Lay Dying	Huckleberry Finn	A Passage to India
As You Like It	I Know Why the Caged	Plato's Republic
The Autobiography of	Bird Sings	Portrait of a Lady
Malcolm X	The Iliad	A Portrait of the Artist
The Awakening	Invisible Man	as a Young Man
Beloved	Jane Eyre	Pride and Prejudice
Beowulf	Jazz	A Raisin in the Sun
Billy Budd	The Joy Luck Club	Richard II
The Bluest Eye, A Novel	Jude the Obscure	Romeo and Juliet
Brave New World	Julius Caesar	The Scarlet Letter
The Canterbury Tales	King Lear	Sir Gawain and the
The Catcher in the Rye	Les Misérables	Green Knight
The Color Purple	Lord of the Flies	Slaughterhouse-Five
The Crucible	Macbeth	Song of Solomon
Death in Venice	The Merchant of Venice	The Sound and the Fury
Death of a Salesman	The Metamorphoses of Ovid	The Stranger
The Divine Comedy I: Inferno	The Metamorphosis	The Sun Also Rises
Dubliners	Middlemarch	A Tale of Two Cities
Emma	A Midsummer Night's Dream	The Taming of the Shrew
Euripides' Medea & Electra	Moby-Dick	The Tempest
Frankenstein	Moll Flanders	Tess of the D'Urbervilles
Gone with the Wind	Mrs. Dalloway	Their Eyes Were Watching God
The Grapes of Wrath	Much Ado About Nothing	To Kill a Mockingbird
Great Expectations	My Antonia	To the Lighthouse
The Great Gatsby	Native Son	Twelfth Night
Gulliver's Travels	1984	Uncle Tom's Cabin
Hamlet	The Odyssey	Waiting for Godot
Hard Times	Oedipus Trilogy	Wuthering Heights

RESEARCH & EDUCATION ASSOCIATION
61 Ethel Road W. • Piscataway, New Jersey 08854
Phone: (908) 819-8880

Please send me more information about MAXnotes®.

Name _____

Address _____

City _____ State _____ Zip _____